AF584931

AUSTRALIAN BUSH SUPERFOODS

PLANT-BASED RECIPES AT HOME

LILY ALICE & THOMAS O'QUINN

Hardie Grant

EXPLORE

FOR ALEXIS AND TOLY

FOR ALL OF YOUR LOVE AND SUPPORT.

We would like to acknowledge that this book has been produced on the traditional land of the Wurundjeri people. We also pay our respects to the many traditional owners of the bushfoods featured from across Australia.

The information we have presented has been prepared with a deep respect for the wisdom and knowledge gathered by Aboriginal people.

We hope this book contributes to a greater understanding and connectedness to the country we share.

CONTENTS

ABOUT THE AUTHORS/ILLUSTRATORS/DESIGNERS

Melbourne-born Lily grew up in Alice Springs, the heart of Australia, where she spent her childhood catching bugs for show-and-tell and avoiding brushing her hair at all costs. Lily went on bush tucker trips with her dad, Toly, and the Anmatyerr ladies from the Utopia community north-east of Alice Springs. They would set out in an earth-smelling, red-dusted troopy and return home with bundles of bush potato (anatye), witchetty grubs (tyarpe) and bush tomato (akayterre). In 2005, Lily moved back to Melbourne to finish school, before completing an Advanced Diploma in Advertising and Graphic Design at Grenadi School of Design. Lily created the botanical illustrations throughout the book.

Thomas was born and educated in Melbourne. It was through a scholastic journey of trial and error, including a brief stint as a landscape gardener, that Thomas found his way to Grenadi School of Design. He spent four years juggling study, full-time work, and writing and performing as a singer-songwriter, graduating with a Diploma of Graphic Design in 2016.

Lily and partner Thomas work together as dreams&bones design. Both avid animal lovers and supporters of animal rights, Thomas and Lily made the switch to a vegan lifestyle several years ago. They found that rather than create limitations, it opened up a whole new world of interesting and nutrient-rich ingredients and has had a profound impact on their health and well-being. They both share a passion for cooking and nutrition, which often finds them clanging around in the kitchen at all hours and serving up experimental concoctions to their friends and family.

www.dreamsandbones.com.au

ABOUT THE MOTIF ARTIST

Dixon Patten is a proud Yorta Yorta and Gunnai man and has family bloodlines from Dhudhuroa, Gunditjmara, Wiradjuri, Yuin, Wemba Wemba, Barapa Barapa and Monaro.

Dixon is an experienced graphic designer and practising artist. Several of his family members have influenced his work and given him knowledge of traditional art practices and stories. Before moving into freelance operation, Dixon was employed by the Koorie Heritage Trust Cultural Centre in Melbourne for eight years. During this time he deepened his understanding of local history and the integral role that art plays in community.

Dixon illustrated the artwork below, which is featured throughout the book. He says of the motif:

"The different leaves represent various plant/food sources from all over Australia. The circle in the middle depicts people/community coming together to partake in ceremony and to eat together. This is universal to mankind – sharing food with others brings comfort, wealth and benefits."

INTRODUCTION

In Indigenous Australian culture, 'Country' is family, the giver and sustainer of life, a land of bountiful resources to be respected and protected, a land of Dreaming; it is all living things.

For at least 50,000 years, Aboriginal and Torres Strait Islander people have lived on this ancient land, many of these communities in its vast arid interior. Yet this seemingly inhospitable continent is home to some of the world's most diverse edible flora, found across the regions, from desert to rainforest. Many of those unique species boast nutritional and medicinal properties not found anywhere else on the planet.

The Kakadu plum, native to the tropical woodlands of the Northern Territory and Western Australia, has unmatched vitamin C content. Bush tomatoes or kutjera, found in the deserts of central Australia, are anti-oxidant rich and a plentiful, portable high-energy hit. Knowledge of these superfoods and others, their astounding health benefits and their many uses, has been passed down in Aboriginal culture for thousands of years.

By definition, superfoods are nutrient-rich foods considered to be especially beneficial for health and well-being. Many of Australia's native bushfoods contain nutritional qualities that not only qualify them as superfoods, but in some cases outshine the more commonly known forms. As people become more interested in healthy eating, many of Australia's bushfoods are finding their way onto the pages of cookbooks, food and health blogs, and into the kitchens of top restaurants all over the world.

Our intention, with this humble little cookbook, is to properly introduce you to the edible natural wonders this country has to offer and provide recipes and inspiration on how to use these exciting new ingredients in your kitchen. Fresh warrigal greens bought at the farmers market, macadamia nuts from your local grocery store, the lemon myrtle bush growing in your very own backyard – the foods that nourished and sustained the first peoples of this land continue to grow and thrive all around us.

This book includes 40 of Australia's most interesting and beneficial bush superfoods, with information on their natural habitat and distribution, traditional uses, nutritional qualities and the best ways to use them, followed by a signature plant-based recipe utilising each ingredient.

A glossary explains some of the less familiar nutritional heroes and base ingredients featured in these recipes – ingredients that form the backbone of much of our cooking. Alternatives and vegetarian substitutes are offered in boxed text in some recipes. Where possible, we have included vegetarian alternatives and substitutes for those looking to include dairy. Most recipes are gluten-free, these recipes appear with an icon.

We've also included a section on sourcing bush superfoods – dried, fresh or frozen – with a guide to seasonality and links to specialist suppliers. We'd urge you to keep your eyes open at farmers markets and food festivals for small operators selling wild-harvested and commercially grown bushfoods. More and more people are recognising the potential in making these ancient ingredients new again.

In showing you how easy it can be to assimilate these superfoods and the health-giving properties attached to them into your daily life in simple, plant-based forms, it is our hope that we may all gain a better understanding of, and connection to, this country that we share.

SOURCING BUSH SUPERFOODS

The best way to get familiar with cooking with bushfoods is to build up a bushfoods pantry. You might start with just a few bushfood ingredients – perhaps dried seeds and herbs – before sourcing fresh and frozen bushfood, and adding them to your kitchen.

Although bushfood ingredients can be a little hard to find, once you've got a variety of native ingredients on hand you will soon see just how easy it is to incorporate the unique and varied flavours of Australia's bushfoods into your everyday cooking.

This section is your guide to the form in which you'll most commonly find these bushfoods, when they're in season and where you can buy them.

FROZEN

ROSELLA

LEMON ASPEN

RIBERRY

FRESH

RIVER MINT

ICE PLANT

KARKALLA

DRIED

STRAWBERRY GUM

QUANDONG

LEMON MYRTLE

FRESH

These bush foods are great to use in recipes when picked straight from the garden or sourced fresh from a supplier.

native basil
bower spinach
native currant
finger lime
native ginger
ice plant
karkalla
lemon aspen
lemon myrtle
lilly pilly
mountain pepper leaf
muntry
munyeroo
river mint
saltbush
samphire
sea parsley
seablite
native thyme
warrigal greens

These fresh greens and herbs can be frozen, but this is only recommended if you plan to use them in cooked meals:

- native basil
- native ginger
- river mint
- saltbush
- sea parsley
- native thyme
- warrigal greens

Finger limes and muntries can be frozen and defrosted before use without compromising form or flavour.

These fresh herbs can be dried in the sun or using a dehydrator:

- native basil
- native ginger
- river mint
- saltbush
- sea parsley
- native thyme

SALT BUSH
FINGER LIME
NATIVE THYME
BOWER SPINACH
ICE PLANT
SAMPHIRE
RIVER MINT
KARKALLA
SEABLITE
SEA PARSLEY

FROZEN

In frozen form, these bush foods will keep for a long time, and can be pulled out of the freezer any time for an easy addition to a meal.

bunya nut
native currant
Davidson plum
desert lime
finger lime
Illawarra plum
Kakadu plum
lemon aspen
lilly pilly
muntry
passionberry
quandong
riberry
rosella
native tamarind

MUNTRY

KAKADU PLUM

LEMON ASPEN

PASSIONBERRY

ILLAWARRA PLUM

DAVIDSON PLUM

BUNYA NUT

ROSELLA

LILLY PILLY

RIBERRY

FINGER LIMF

DESERT LIME

DRIED

These bush foods are often found in dried form, which is a popular way of preserving their unique flavours for use in dishes all year-round.

anise myrtle
native basil
cinnamon myrtle
gumbi gumbi
Kakadu plum
kutjera
lemon myrtle
macadamia nut
mountain pepper berry & leaf
muntry
passionberry
peppermint gum
quandong
rosella
saltbush
sandalwood nut
strawberry gum
native thyme
wattleseed

PEPPERMINT GUM
KUTJERA
ROSELLA
MOUNTAIN PEPPER
LEMON MYRTLE
NATIVE BASIL
GUMBI GUMBI
MACADAMIA NUT
QUANDONG
WATTLESEED
SANDALWOOD NUT
STRAWBERRY GUM
CINNAMON MYRTLE

WHERE TO BUY BUSH SUPERFOODS

While bushfoods are popping up in more and more markets, supermarkets, delis and health food stores, we easily sourced most of our ingredients online from a variety of bushfood stockists. It is always such a treat receiving a big delivery of these beautiful foods in the mail!

Bushfood Australia
Specialises in whole and milled, wild-harvested wattleseed, quandong, mountain pepper, bush tomato and strawberry gum. Delivers Australia-wide.
www.bushfoodaustralia.com

The Lime Caviar Company
This Queensland company grows and sells fresh and frozen finger limes. Delivers Australia-wide and internationally.
www.limecaviar.net

Outback Chef
Outback Chef offers a wide selection of herbs, spices, teas, fruits, nuts and pastes. Delivers Australia-wide.
www.outbackchef.com.au

Outback Pride Fresh
The Outback Pride Project propagates and cultivates many different bushfood species. This project assists a number of production sites within Aboriginal communities.

Check their website for a full distributor list or to order online. We buy their products through The Vegetable Connection in Fitzroy, Melbourne.
www.outbackpridefresh.com.au

Roogenic
Roogenic has a great range of bush teas and spices and proudly supports local farmers and Aboriginal communities by buying and promoting their products. Delivers Australia-wide.
www.roogenic.com.au

Taste Australia Bush Food Shop

Taste Australia Bush Food Shop is an online store based in south-east Queensland that stocks a wide selection of dried, bottled and frozen bushfoods. Delivers Australia-wide. www.bushfoodshop.com.au

Health food stores

Try visiting health food stores if you're looking for Kakadu plum powder, macadamia nuts and bush teas.

Supermarkets

You'll commonly find wattleseed, macadamia nuts, lemon myrtle, mountain pepper, bush spices and fresh finger limes (in season) at supermarkets.

SEASONALITY

Different bush foods become plentiful at certain times of the year. Keep in mind seasonality when looking for fresh versions of these plants, whether you are planning to use them in fresh form, or wanting to preserve them in dried or frozen form.

YEAR-ROUND

bower spinach
native currant
karkalla
munyeroo
river mint
saltbush
sea parsley
seablite
native thyme
warrigal greens

SUMMER

native basil
finger lime
ice plant
lemon myrtle
mountain pepper leaf
muntry
samphire

AUTUMN

native basil
samphire

WINTER

ice plant
lilly pilly

SPRING

native basil
finger lime
ice plant
lemon aspen
lemon myrtle
mountain pepper leaf
samphire

ANISE MYRTLE

Syzygium anisatum

A close relative of lemon myrtle (*Backhousia citriodora*), the anise myrtle tree is known not just for its beautiful, fluffy white blossoms but also, and perhaps more so, for the glossy, green liquorice-scented leaves it bears.

Known in the past as aniseed myrtle but changed to anise to avoid confusion with the aniseed of the *Apiaceae* family, the anise myrtle, or ringwood as it is otherwise known, is native to the rainforests of southern Queensland and northern New South Wales, where it can grow up to 45 metres tall. Though now quite rare in the wild, anise myrtle is commercially grown across New South Wales and Queensland, primarily for the essential oil yielded from its leaves.

Traditionally used by Indigenous Australians to make a vitalising tonic, battle-weary soldiers of WWII also utilised the leaves of the anise myrtle to make a similar energy-boosting concoction. It was also used as a bush remedy for stomach aches and is said to have helped improve lactation in breastfeeding mothers.

Anise myrtle leaves have one of the highest known concentrations of anethole, a compound with potent antibacterial, antifungal and antiviral properties that gives anise myrtle its unique liquorice flavour and aroma. The leaves are also rich in antioxidants, calcium, magnesium, vitamins A, C and E, and lutein, also known as the 'eye vitamin'.

Similar to star anise in flavour, and with its aniseed-like smell, anise myrtle lends a unique, delicious note to both savoury and sweet recipes such as marinades, salad dressings and dessert sauces. The dried leaves can also be infused to make an invigorating, refreshing herbal tea. Anise myrtle may be sourced as an essential oil or in dried leaf form year-round.

ANISE MYRTLE YOYO BISCUITS

MAKES 8-10

Anise myrtle lends a mellow liquorice flavour that complements the fresh lemon zest in the biscuits and the creamy filling.

Biscuits

2 cups almond flour
⅓ cup rice malt syrup
½ teaspoon gluten-free baking powder
1 teaspoon vanilla extract
2 teaspoons grated lemon zest
2 teaspoons dried anise myrtle

Lemon cream

grated zest and juice of 1 lemon
½ cup raw cashews (soaked for at least 30 minutes)
1 tablespoon rice malt syrup
1 teaspoon dried anise myrtle

Preheat the oven to 175°C (340°F) and line a baking tray with baking paper.

In a large bowl, mix the almond flour, rice malt syrup, baking powder, vanilla extract, lemon zest and anise myrtle until the mixture forms a dough. Use your hands to roll small pieces of dough into balls about 2 cm in diameter. Place them on the baking tray, about 4 cm apart. Use a fork to gently flatten each ball and leave the characteristic tine pattern.

Bake in the oven for 15 minutes, or until a little golden. Set aside to cool completely on a rack.

To make the lemon cream, add the lemon zest and juice, cashews, rice malt syrup and anise myrtle to a blender and blend until smooth.

To assemble the yoyos, spread lemon cream onto the flat side of a biscuit. Top with another biscuit and gently press together. Repeat. Yoyos will keep in an airtight container for up to 3 days and can be frozen.

NATIVE BASIL

Although it can be mistaken for a weed, it is the sweet basil aroma that is the trademark of this naturalised herb. An intensely aromatic plant, native basil is a compact and adaptable shrub with a number of medicinal and culinary uses.

Believed to have been introduced to Australia hundreds of years ago by Indonesian traders, this close relative of holy basil, also known in Australia as bush tea leaf, is a widespread herb that thrives in the arid, rugged terrain of northern Queensland and the Northern Territory. Native basil is now commercially grown in native plant nurseries for home gardens and is available from a variety of bushfood stockists, fresh and dried.

The Indigenous people of Australia have long employed the medicinal benefits of native basil, using it to create an antibacterial paste that would be applied to wounds and skin infections and drunk as a healing tea. Native basil has also been important in ceremonial use, particularly in smoking ceremonies in which the leaves would be placed over hot coals to create a smoke used to rid people or places of bad energies. Aboriginal women have used native basil as a natural perfume by crushing the leaves and rubbing them onto their skin.

Native basil shares many of the same nutritional qualities as holy basil, including a rich concentration of vitamins A and C, calcium, zinc, iron and chlorophyll, beneficial in red blood cell production. As well as having antibacterial, antimicrobial and anti-inflammatory properties, native basil is also reported to have cancer-fighting attributes.

Native basil can be used in much the same way as common culinary basil, adding a more complex herbal dimension to dishes. It is a particularly delicious base for pesto and can be added to pasta sauces, soups and tomato-based recipes. It can also be made into a refreshing, calming tea, when steeped in hot water for a few minutes. Native basil is available dried year-round and fresh between September and May. If bought fresh, native basil may be dried or frozen for later use.

ZUCCHINI NOODLES WITH NATIVE BASIL PESTO

SERVES 2-4

Zucchini 'noodles' are a lighter, seasonal alternative to regular noodles or pasta. In this recipe we use the zucchini raw, keeping its shape and bite. The native basil adds a strong herbaceous flavour to the pesto. Be sure to make more than enough of the native basil pesto for later use.

- 1 cup native basil, fresh, leaves and stem
- 1 cup kale, leaves finely chopped, stems discarded
- 2 garlic cloves
- ½ cup olive oil
- 3 tablespoons nutritional yeast
- 2 tablespoons lemon juice
- pinch of salt (optional)
- 1 cup macadamia nuts
- 2 zucchini
- 1 handful cherry tomatoes, quartered to garnish

To make the pesto, blend the basil, kale, garlic, olive oil, nutritional yeast, lemon juice and salt in a blender until combined.

Toast the macadamia nuts in a dry frying pan over a medium heat for 3-5 minutes or until lightly golden. Watch and stir frequently as the nuts can easily burn. Leave to cool slightly, then coarsely crush the nuts using a mortar and pestle and add to the pesto.

Using a vegetable spiraliser, vegetable peeler, julienne peeler or mandoline slicer, create the zucchini noodles.

Serve the zucchini noodles topped with pesto and cherry tomatoes.

NOTE

Try using left-over pesto on baked potatoes, add a dollop to soup, as a sandwich spread, or serve as a dip with crackers or chopped-up veggies.

BOWER SPINACH

Tetragonia implexicoma

Also known as barilla or Coorong spinach and a close relative of warrigal greens, this rambling, low-growing native plant was identified early as a valuable source of vitamin C. In the late 18th century, specimens of bower spinach were one of many Australian plants sent back to collections, institutions and private gardens in Britain and France and were common table greens.

Native to both New Zealand and Australia, this wildly adaptive plant can be found in just about every Australian state and territory, particularly favouring the coastal environments of south-eastern Australia where it grows in dense masses along its beaches and dunes. Like its ice plant relative, bower spinach is grown commercially in boxes of composted seaweed.

A valued green vegetable to the Aboriginal people of Australia, its succulent, salty leaves were commonly gathered and eaten raw or cooked and eaten as an addition to other meals. Bower spinach's edible, bright-red berries also provided a sweet treat and, when crushed and mixed with water, a valuable red dye.

Like warrigal greens, bower spinach is a good source of vitamin C and antioxidants. The plump leaves contain anti-ulcerogenic and anti-inflammatory properties as well as caffeic acid, a chemical found in various plants and foods that is used to boost athletic performance, aid in weight loss and has been shown to reduce the growth of certain cancer cells.

Bower spinach is similar to English spinach, but with a thicker texture and distinct salty flavour; it is used in much the same way as common spinach. It may be eaten fresh or blanched briefly and makes a great addition to soups, pasta sauces or pies. It's sustainably grown and is reliably available fresh year-round.

BOWER SPINACH & CANNELLINI SOUP

SERVES 4

This hearty soup utilises the succulent leaves of bower spinach in a quick and delicious recipe perfect for the winter months.

1 tablespoon olive oil
2 leeks, white parts finely chopped
1 fennel bulb, finely chopped
3 garlic cloves, crushed
1 green chilli, finely chopped
½ cup white wine
2 × 400 g tinned cannellini beans, rinsed and drained
3 sprigs native thyme
2 cups bower spinach leaves and kale leaves removed from stem
1 tablespoon apple cider vinegar
1 bay leaf
5 cups vegetable stock
micro herbs and lemon wedges, to garnish (optional)
gluten-free toast (optional)

Heat the olive oil in a large stockpot over medium heat and sauté the leek and fennel until soft, about 5 minutes. Add the garlic and chilli and cook for a further minute. Add the white wine and cook until the wine has just about evaporated, about 5 minutes.

Add the cannellini beans, native thyme, bower spinach, kale, vinegar, bay leaf and stock to the pot and cook at a low simmer for a further 20 minutes. Top with the micro herbs, if using, and serve immediately.

BUNYA NUT

Araucaria bidwillii

For thousands of years the nut of the bunya pine has carried greater significance to the Aboriginal people of Australia than that of just a bushfood; to this day, it remains a symbol of peace and celebration.

Bunya pines have a dense conical canopy, with plated green seed cones that grow bigger than a pineapple. Within these 5–10 kilogram cones grow masses of the edible nuts. The trees, which have been known to grow up to a staggering 80 metres tall in the wild, are endemic to the subtropical rainforests of south-east Queensland and northern New South Wales and are especially abundant around the Bunya Mountains, an area of great cultural importance to the Aboriginal people of the region. Bunya pines are grown commercially and wild-harvested for their nuts and timber, the latter particularly favoured in the making of guitars.

Aboriginal clans from near and far would gather in the Bunya region of southern Queensland when the harvests of bunya nuts were most bountiful, every three or four years. A great feast would be held and intertribal activities would take place, including sports, exchanges of knowledge, marriage arrangements and the settling of disputes. Excess nuts would be buried underground in mud to preserve them for later consumption.

Nutritionally similar to chestnuts, bunya nuts are rich in dietary fibre, protein, healthy oils, unsaturated fats and complex carbohydrates, as well as the minerals potassium and magnesium. Studies have also found that bunya nuts contain antibacterial properties, and research is being undertaken into its potential use as a preservative.

Similar to chestnuts in flavour as well, bunya nuts have a nutty pine flavour and waxy texture and can readily be used as a meat substitute. The nut meat is also a tasty alternative to potatoes in soups and curries and makes a delicious nut butter. Roasted and ground, bunya nuts can also be used as a particularly binding gluten-free flour. Bunya nuts are usually sold still in their hard shell. The best way to prepare the nuts is to cook them in boiling water for around 30 minutes, or place them in a hot oven for the same amount of time; either method will make them much easier to open. The nuts may be sourced fresh when in season but are most commonly available frozen.

BUNYA NUT BORSCHT

SERVES 4-6

This is a time-tested and much-loved recipe handed down from Lily's babushka. While the original recipe calls for the addition of potatoes, this version uses bunya nuts, which provide a similar starchy texture and a subtle nutty taste.

- 10 bunya nuts (see note)
- 1 whole onion, peeled, ends trimmed
- 2½ litres vegetable stock
- 4 bay leaves
- 3 large or 4 small beetroots, peeled and diced
- 2 carrots, roughly chopped
- 6 large tomatoes, chopped
- 2 × 400 g tinned butterbeans
- 1 cup cabbage, shredded
- freshly chopped spring onions or coriander
- salt and pepper

Cashew sour cream

- 1 cup raw cashews (soaked for at least 30 minutes)
- ¼ cup water
- ½ teaspoon apple cider vinegar
- 1 teaspoon lemon juice
- pinch of salt and pepper

ALTERNATIVELY

Sour cream can be used in place of the cashew cream.

Put a large stockpot of salted water on to boil.

To soften the bunya nut shells, add the nuts to the boiling water and simmer for 30–40 minutes or until the nut shell has softened. Drain and let cool.

To remove the shell of the bunya nut, carefully cut the shell lengthways with secateurs and remove the nut within. Cut the nuts into quarters and put aside.

In the same stockpot, put the whole onion with the vegetable stock and bay leaves. Bring to the boil, then reduce the heat and simmer for 10 minutes.

Add the beetroot, carrots, tomatoes and bunya nuts to the stock and simmer for 5 minutes. Drain and rinse the butterbeans, then add to the pot, along with the shredded cabbage. Cook for a further 15 minutes, or until the beetroot is cooked through. Season generously with salt and freshly ground black pepper.

Meanwhile, make the cashew cream by combining all the ingredients in a blender and blending for 1–2 minutes or until smooth.

Serve the borscht topped with a spoonful of cashew cream, sliced spring onions, coriander or your favourite fresh herb.

NOTE

Bunya nuts are usually sold still in their hard shell. These underrated nuts are a bit of a challenge to get to but boiling them in water helps to soften the shell for removal. You will need a heavy knife, scissors or even secateurs.

CINNAMON MYRTLE

Backhousia myrtifolia

Another member of the *Myrtaceae* family that found fame with lemon myrtle and anise myrtle for its culinary potential, the oil-rich, glossy green leaves and timber of the cinnamon myrtle tree have long been used in traditional Aboriginal culture.

This small rainforest tree, with cream flowers surrounded by a puff of wispy stamens, pink tipped after flowering, is widespread amongst the subtropical rainforests of northern New South Wales and Queensland. Though small in stature, the cinnamon myrtle tree is also known as ironwood and never break, due to its incredibly tough wood. Cinnamon myrtle has long been a popular garden plant for its beautiful flowers and aromatic foliage and is widely sold in native plant nurseries.

Indigenous Australians treasured the wood of the cinnamon myrtle for its strength and durability, commonly using it to make tools and weapons. The aromatic leaves were used medicinally to treat upset stomachs and cold symptoms, infused in water and drunk, and also acted as a natural insect repellent when crushed and rubbed onto the skin.

Today, cinnamon myrtle is used in much the same ways as old, commonly brewed to make a soothing medicinal tea said to alleviate symptoms of heartburn, indigestion and other digestive problems. The main essential oil in cinnamon myrtle is elemicin, an organic compound also found in nutmeg, and is known for its antiseptic, antimicrobial, anti-inflammatory, antibacterial and analgesic properties.

The aroma and flavour of cinnamon myrtle is indeed cinnamon-like with a hint of bubblegum and can be used anywhere that regular cinnamon is called for. Use whole leaf in the same way as a bay leaf in curries, stews and pasta sauces and add ground to dessert recipes such as biscuits and brownies to impart a mild, warm cinnamon flavour. A soothing tea can be made by adding dried leaves to boiling water and steeping for 5–7 minutes.

Cinnamon myrtle leaves may be used fresh if you can source them but are more widely available dried, ground, or as part of herbal tea blends.

CINNAMON MYRTLE SPICED ROAST CHICKPEA SALAD

SERVES 2

This is one of our easy, go-to weekday meals that is substantial enough to be served on its own.

Spiced roast chickpeas

400 g tinned chickpeas
1 teaspoon garlic powder
1 teaspoon ground cinnamon myrtle
¼ teaspoon ground cumin
1 teaspoon sweet paprika
½ teaspoon salt
1 tablespoon olive oil

Tahini & lemon dressing

4 tablespoons tahini
1 garlic clove, crushed
1 tablespoon maple syrup
grated zest and juice of 1 lemon
¼ cup water

Salad

1 avocado, thinly sliced
2 cups baby spinach, roughly chopped
handful of coriander leaves, roughly chopped
3 spring onions, sliced
1 cup cherry tomatoes, quartered

Preheat the oven to 200°C (400°F) and line a baking tray with baking paper.

Drain the chickpeas and combine with the garlic powder, cinnamon myrtle, cumin, paprika, salt and olive oil in a large bowl. Mix until the chickpeas are well coated, then spread evenly onto the baking tray. Roast for 30 minutes, turning once.

To make the tahini and lemon dressing, whisk all the ingredients in a small bowl until well combined.

Combine the warm spiced chickpeas, avocado, baby spinach, coriander, spring onions and cherry tomatoes in a large bowl and serve with the tahini and lemon dressing.

NATIVE CURRANT

Acrotriche depressa

This prickly native shrub – with its fleshy red-purple berries – has become such a rarity in the wild that it was believed to be extinct in Victoria until it was rediscovered there in 2009.

Also known as wiry ground-berry, this low-growing plant was once commonly found in the sandy and dense clay soils of southern South Australia, ranging from the Adelaide Hills to Kangaroo Island, where it can still be found growing today. While native currant is considered to be endangered in the wild, it is now commercially grown, ensuring availability of its berries year-round.

The attractive fruits of the native currant were particularly favoured by early Aboriginal people for their sweet and tangy juice and were commonly eaten straight from the tree. The flowers were also sucked of their nectar and steeped in water to make a sweet, refreshing drink.

Native currants are not only a valuable source of vitamin C but are also rich in polyphenol antioxidants, naturally occurring plant-based compounds that have been shown to promote healthy blood sugar levels, reduce inflammation, improve heart health and defend against certain cancers.

The fruit of the native currant is similar in flavour to the common red- or blackcurrant but with more tartness and acidity. Because of the inedible hard seed within, it is best to extract the juice of the berries by blending them, then straining the juice. Due to the acidity of the berries, it is better balanced out with sugar and therefore works particularly well in sweet recipes such as jams, dessert sauces and cocktails. Native currants are available year-round in fresh and frozen form.

NATIVE CURRANT SWIRL MUFFINS

MAKES 10

The swirls of tangy native currant syrup pair beautifully with the lemon zest of these muffins. If you make a double quantity of syrup, you can use it on pancakes or pour a dash over roasting carrots or pumpkin.

Native currant syrup

2 cups native currants, fresh or frozen, plus extra to garnish
1 cup water
1–2 tablespoons rice malt syrup

Muffins

½ cup almond milk
½ cup lemon juice
1 tablespoon flaxseed meal
4 cups almond flour
½ teaspoon gluten-free baking powder
½ teaspoon gluten-free baking soda
½ cup maple syrup
1 tablespoon grated lemon zest, plus extra to garnish
1 teaspoon vanilla extract
1 tablespoon coconut oil

ALTERNATIVELY

1 egg can be used instead of flaxseed meal.

Use your milk preference instead of almond milk.

Preheat the oven to 180°C (350°F). Lightly grease 10 large muffin moulds – we use silicone moulds, which makes the muffins much easier to get out.

To make the syrup, combine the native currants and water in a small saucepan and bring to the boil. Gently simmer for 5 minutes, then strain off most of the water. Transfer the currants to a sieve over a bowl and press with the back of a tablespoon to drain the juice and remove the seeds. Stir the rice malt syrup into the currant juice and set aside.

Place the almond milk, lemon juice and flaxseed meal into a large bowl, mix well and allow to sit for 5–10 minutes so the mixture thickens slightly. Mix in the almond flour, baking powder, baking soda, maple syrup, lemon zest, vanilla extract and coconut oil.

Spoon the mixture into the muffin moulds, then gently swirl 2–3 teaspoons of the syrup into the top of each muffin without completely mixing the syrup into the batter. Bake for 30–35 minutes or until the muffins are golden brown around the edges. Remove from the oven and cool on a rack for a few minutes before removing them from the moulds.

Garnish with the extra native currants and lemon zest.

DAVIDSON PLUM

Davidsonia pruriens

Affectionately referred to as the queen of Australian rainforest 'plums', the fleshy, purple-blue fruit of the Davidson plum tree, or ooray, is fast becoming one of Australia's most sought-after native superfoods, with an estimated 12–15 tonnes of this vibrant, tangy fruit produced in commercial cultivation annually.

All four varieties of Davidson plum favour the tropical zones of eastern Australia and can be found growing in the rainforests of northern Queensland through to New South Wales, though they are quite rare in the wild today. The tree grows to 10 metres, with the deeply coloured fruit growing in clusters on the trunk.

Though not commonly eaten fresh today due to its extremely sour taste, traditional owners were particularly fond of the fruit's tangy flavour and readily ate it freshly plucked from the tree. The wood was also a valued resource, with the trunk used to make tools and weapons such as harpoons for fishing.

Rich in anthocyanins that give Davidson plums their deep purple colour and bright crimson flesh, they're loaded with naturally occurring antioxidants, that aid in protecting the body from the harmful effects of free radicals, boasting a higher antioxidant content than blueberries. This versatile fruit is also high in folate, zinc, magnesium, calcium, phosphorus, potassium, manganese, copper and lutein, a carotenoid vitamin proven to help prevent macular degeneration and cataracts.

Davidson plums have a tart flavour similar to a satsuma, with a fruity, earthy aroma reminiscent of beetroot. Due to the low sugar content of Davidson plums, they are best utilised in jams and dessert sauces. Their fruity tang also works fantastically in savoury dishes as a marinade or alongside as a chutney. Davidson plums may be difficult to source fresh; however, they are available in frozen form year-round.

DAVIDSON PLUM CHILLI SAUCE

MAKES 1 CUP

This sweet and sour sauce goes well with just about anything in need of a dipping sauce and goes particularly well with our Warrigal Greens & Kale Pie (page 176).

2 cups Davidson plums, fresh or frozen, finely diced
4 garlic cloves, finely chopped
1 long red chilli, finely chopped
1 teaspoon freshly grated ginger
2 tablespoons apple cider vinegar
1 teaspoon tamari or soy sauce
rice malt syrup to taste

Combine all the ingredients in a medium-sized non-reactive saucepan and simmer over a low heat for 20 minutes, stirring occasionally. Stir in ⅓ cup of water and let cool.

Pour the sauce into sterilised jars. It will keep well for a month; refrigerate once opened.

DESERT LIME

Citrus glauca

This remarkably adaptive native citrus is undoubtedly one of Australia's hardiest bushfoods, with the ability to thrive in some of the country's most extreme temperatures. Bearing fruit resembling tiny lemons – but with an intense lime flavour – it has served as a zesty and delicious thirst-quencher for many a parched wanderer for thousands of years.

Able to withstand temperatures as low as 4°C and as high as 45°C, the desert lime is not only resistant to conditions of extreme heat and frost, but is also tolerant of drought and saline conditions. This thorny shrub naturally occurs in the dry, inland regions of southern Queensland and western New South Wales across to the Flinders Ranges of South Australia. Commercial cultivation of the desert lime was set up in the early 1990s.

With its very thin skin, the desert lime does not require peeling and can be eaten straight from the tree, a fact widely known by Indigenous Australians, who would eat the tangy, bitter fruits raw as a source of immune-boosting vitamins and to quench their thirst on hot days.

Though small in size – the fruit only grows to around the size of a large grape – desert limes pack a serious nutritional punch. They have three times the vitamin C content found in oranges and are high in vitamin E, folate, calcium and lutein. Desert limes also possess a high potassium to sodium ratio, which may aid in stabilising blood sugar levels and lowering blood pressure.

Desert limes have a piquant flavour and a true citrus aroma. The flesh and juice can be used in much the same way as regular limes or lemons, lending themselves to tangy conserves, chutneys, desserts and drinks. Desert limes are available year-round in frozen, dried, and powdered form, and if sourced fresh, can be frozen for later use without losing flavour or form.

DESERT LIME CHEESECAKES

MAKES 6

These no-bake cheesecakes are a quick and incredibly easy way to utilise the delicious tang of desert limes.

Base

1 cup raw macadamia nuts
⅓ cup desiccated coconut
5 dates, pitted

Filling

1 avocado
200 g raw cashews (soaked for at least 30 minutes)
40 desert limes
1 teaspoon vanilla extract
¼ cup pure maple syrup
1 tablespoon coconut oil
2 teaspoons dried lemon myrtle
2 teaspoons matcha powder (optional)
lime zest, to garnish

Lightly oil a 6-hole giant muffin tin using coconut oil. We use a silicone mould to make it a little easier to get the cheesecakes out once frozen.

To make the base, pulse the raw macadamias, desiccated coconut and dates in a blender until well combined.

Spoon the macadamia nut mixture into the muffin tin and flatten with the base of a glass, filling to about ⅓ of each hole. Cover and place in the freezer.

To make the filling, blitz all the ingredients in a blender until smooth and creamy. We like to add 2 teaspoons of matcha powder to really boost the beautiful green colour of these cheesecakes, but it's completely optional.

Take the cheesecake bases out of the freezer and carefully spoon over the filling. Cover again and put back in the freezer for at least 3 hours.

About 15–20 minutes before serving, remove from the freezer and let sit. Top the cheesecakes with a little freshly grated lime zest.

FINGER LIME

Microcitrus australasica

Of the many botanical wonders the Australian bush has to offer, there are perhaps none quite as delicately beautiful as the Australian finger lime. Dubbed 'lime caviar' in culinary circles for the caviar-like juice vesicles within, the finger lime has quickly become one of Australia's most highly prized bushfoods for its dazzling array of colours and uses in cooking.

Highly susceptible to sunburn and wind, this understorey tree, and the delicate fruit it bears, is native to the subtropical rainforests of south-east Queensland and north-east New South Wales, though now dwindling in its natural habitat due to land development and farming. Finger limes are now grown commercially and in home gardens as the demand for this exotic-looking bushfood continues to rise with finger limes appearing in the kitchens of many top restaurants both at home and abroad.

The fruit of the finger lime has been utilised by the Aboriginal peoples of Australia as both a food source and bush medicine for thousands of years. While the juicy flesh provided a burst of flavour and immunity-boosting nutrients, a concoction of the pulp was also used as a natural antiseptic that would be applied to infected cuts and boils.

Like all citrus fruits, finger limes are a fantastic source of vitamin C and flavonoids, powerful antioxidants with anti-inflammatory benefits and immune-boosting properties. The finger lime is also a great source of potassium, an essential mineral known to aid in lowering blood pressure and boost the nervous system.

Finger limes have a zesty-citrus aroma and a wonderful tangy but sweet flavour similar to a lemon or lime – but more intense. The unique bead-like cells of the finger lime – with yellow, red, pink, purple and pale green varieties – make a stunning decorative addition to dishes both savoury and sweet such as sushi, cheesecake, cocktails and anywhere regular lime is called for. Finger limes are available fresh and frozen – they can be frozen for up to 12 months without loss of form or flavour. They are also available in dried, powdered form.

SWEET POTATO TOAST WITH FINGER LIME GUACAMOLE

SERVES 2

Just slice uncooked sweet potato lengthways – no more than ½ cm thick – and pop it into the toaster at maximum setting. The finger limes are available in beautiful shades of green to red and add delicious, tangy pops of flavour to this guacamole

- 2 avocados
- 6 finger limes
- handful of chopped coriander leaves, plus extra to garnish
- ½ green chilli, finely diced (more or less, depending on heat preference)
- pinch of salt and pepper
- 1–2 large sweet potatoes
- extra finger limes, sliced, to garnish (optional)
- extra green chilli, sliced, to garnish (optional)

To make the guacamole, cut the avocados in half and scoop the flesh into a large bowl. Roughly mash using a fork or potato masher.

Cut the finger limes in half and squeeze out the vesicles into a bowl, saving some for garnish. Add in the coriander, chilli, salt and pepper and stir to combine.

Slice the sweet potato lengthways into ½ cm thick pieces. Put the slices into the toaster, at maximum setting, and toast until soft. If you're cooking double quantities, it's probably easier to cook the sweet potato under the grill until soft.

Spread the smashed avocado onto the sweet potato toast and serve with chopped coriander, green chilli and lime slices if using.

NATIVE GINGER

Alpinia caerulea

Of the same family as common ginger, this native perennial herb with long, glossy green leaves and bright blue berries also grows from a nutrient-rich rhizome and has multiple edible parts. The sweet, seedy pulp of the edible berries is used by bushwalkers to encourage saliva production and moisten the mouth while on long hikes.

From the genus *Alpinia*, which contains over 230 species, this adaptable cane-like shrub is vulnerable to drought and frost conditions, instead preferring the warm and shady settings of subtropical north-east Queensland and central New South Wales. Most commonly cultivated in gardens for its ornamental qualities, native ginger is also grown in small- to medium-scale bushfood nurseries for its edible seeds, roots, leaves and fruits.

As with many of Australia's bushfoods, Aboriginal people made full use of this versatile plant. The young rhizome shoots were particularly favoured for their sweet, gingery flavour while the berries were sucked for their sour pulp, with the seeds generally discarded. It is believed that these seeds were used to mark trails for navigational use. The aromatic leaves were used to line earth ovens and wrap foods such as fish to impart a mild ginger flavour while cooking. The strappy leaves were also woven and used to make thatched shelters.

The dark blue berries of native ginger are exceptionally high in calcium, iron and magnesium and are a valuable source of zinc, phosphorus and copper. The edible rhizome contains high levels of essential vitamins and minerals such as magnesium, potassium, copper, manganese and vitamins B and C.

Even though the whole plant is edible, it is the leaves of native ginger that are most commonly available. The leaves have a mild flavour and aroma of ginger and work well added to curries, laksas and soups, or they can be used to wrap food prior to baking or roasting. A refreshing, digestive tea can also be made by steeping dried leaves in hot water for 2–3 minutes. Native ginger leaves are available fresh year-round, freeze well and are easily dried.

GREEN CURRY WITH NATIVE GINGER LEAF

SERVES 4

The mild ginger taste of the native ginger leaf really complements the citrus flavours in this creamy curry. We've made this recipe a little less spicy than your conventional green curry – just add more chilli if you prefer yours with a bit more heat. Any extra curry paste can be used in a stir-fry.

Green curry paste

1 native ginger leaf, chopped, fresh or frozen
½–1 green chilli, roughly chopped
2 tablespoons lemongrass, white part only, finely chopped
½ cup shallots, chopped
3 garlic cloves, chopped
1 tablespoon freshly grated ginger
½ cup fresh coriander
1 teaspoon ground coriander
2 tablespoons tamari or soy
¼ cup lime juice or 10 whole desert limes
3 kaffir lime leaves, stems removed, finely chopped
1 cup fresh basil
¼ cup coconut milk

Curry

1 tablespoon coconut oil
1 onion, finely diced
2 garlic cloves, crushed
1 cup Green Curry Paste
2 cups coconut milk
2 cups vegetable stock
1 whole native ginger leaf
1 zucchini, diced
1 red capsicum, deseeded and chopped
1 carrot, diced
1 cup green beans, chopped
1½ tablespoons tamari or soy sauce
½ cup snow peas, chopped
1 tablespoon lime juice
coriander leaves, chopped, to garnish

To make the curry paste, place all the ingredients into a blender and blitz until smooth.

To make the curry, heat the coconut oil in a large saucepan over medium heat and add the onion. Sauté gently for about five minutes or until the onion is translucent. Add the garlic and green curry paste and cook for a further minute, until aromatic. Add the coconut milk, stock, native ginger leaf, zucchini, capsicum, carrots, green beans, and tamari or soy sauce. Cook for 20 minutes at a low simmer. Add the snow peas and lime juice and cook for a final minute. Season to taste.

Serve with quinoa or rice and garnish with fresh coriander leaves.

GUMBI GUMBI

Pittosporum angustifolium

Also known as native apricot for the vibrant orange fruit it bears, this small, unassuming tree, with its long slender leaves and willow-like branches, is one of Australia's most potent and culturally important bush medicine plants.

Resistant to severe drought and frost, this resilient and slow-growing mallee tree is found across most of inland Australia, particularly in South Australia and north-western Victoria, but never in large numbers.

Used primarily for its medicinal properties, Indigenous Australians would create a concoction made up of the seeds, fruit pulp and leaves of the gumbi gumbi, ingested for cramp and cold-symptom relief. This same mixture could be applied topically to treat eczema and other skin conditions. The seeds were also ground into flour to make damper. Warmed gumbi gumbi leaves, when pressed against the breasts of new mothers, was believed to induce milk flow.

Recognising its significance as a traditional bush medicine, in 2013 the University of Southern Queensland established the Gumbi Gumbi Gardens, a 2.2 hectare garden in Toowoomba, featuring plantations of gumbi gumbi and more than 100 other plant species used by local Aboriginal communities as food and medicine.

Extensive research is now being done into the medicinal qualities of gumbi gumbi, with impressive results. As well as being an effective treatment for various skin conditions and internal pains, it appears gumbi gumbi has powerful cancer-fighting properties together with antispasmodic, antiviral, antioxidant and anti-inflammatory agents.

The leaves of gumbi gumbi have a slightly bitter, eucalyptus flavour and are best enjoyed brewed into a relaxing herbal tea. Gumbi gumbi leaves are available year-round powdered, whole dried and capsulated, as well as in the form of essential oil.

GUMBI GUMBI & PEPPERMINT GUM ICED TEA

MAKES 1 L

This tasty and naturally sweet health tonic is fantastic served with ice on a hot summer's day, or hot and freshly brewed.

- 30 dried gumbi gumbi leaves
- 4 tablespoons dried liquorice root
- 4 teaspoons dried peppermint gum
- ice, to serve
- fresh river mint, finely chopped, to serve

Bring 1 litre of water to the boil in a large saucepan. Add the gumbi gumbi leaves and reduce heat to a low boil, simmering for 12 minutes. Add the liquorice root and simmer for another 5 minutes, giving everything a stir from time to time. Sprinkle in the peppermint gum leaves and boil for a final 3 minutes.

Turn off the heat, then add an additional cup of water. Strain the tea into a jug with a lid and let chill in the fridge overnight.

Serve with ice cubes and fresh sprigs of river mint.

NOTE

The liquorice root provides a natural sweetness to the tea, but feel free to add your own preferred sweetener if you'd like to sweeten it further.

ICE PLANT

Mesembryanthemum crystallinum

Highly sought after by chefs for use as a decorative garnish due to the amazing crystal-like appearance of the leaves, this creeping succulent owes its name to the glistening, salt-retaining bladder cells that cover the plant, giving it its frozen appearance. It is sometimes known as crystal ice plant.

While this drought- and salt-tolerant succulent is native to Africa, Egypt and Europe, it is naturalised in Australia and can be found in saline areas of Western Australia and southern areas of the country, growing in sandbanks and seaweed deposits. It is, however, something of a rarity in the wild and has found more success in private cultivation, where it grows well in boxes of composted seaweed alongside bower spinach and warrigal greens.

Although there is little documented use of ice plant by Indigenous Australians, it is believed that it was used not just as bushfood, but as a potent bush medicine as well. Contemporary use of the plant began in the 1990s when a German nurse discovered its ability, specifically the sap, to soothe dry skin. The gel yielded incredible results when added to baths to soothe a wide array of skin conditions and has led to the ice plant being used commercially in some skin care products.

As well as being a valuable source of vitamin C, ice plant is also a known diuretic – it helps to rid the body of excess salt and fluid, which in turn lowers blood pressure and can improve cardiovascular health overall. Ice plant is also known for its natural demulcent qualities, making it an effective anti-inflammatory for certain irritated membranes.

Featured heavily in Japanese cooking, ice plant is similar in flavour to English spinach with a crispier texture and salty taste. Like spinach, its leaves work fantastically when steamed, stir-fried or blanched and can be used in pies, salads or as an exceptionally beautiful garnish. Ice plant is only commercially available fresh; leaves can be sourced during the summer, winter and spring months.

RAINBOW SALAD WITH ICE PLANT

SERVES 2

The fresh ice plant adds a savoury, salty dimension to this vibrant, wholesome salad.

- 5 baby beetroots, trimmed and scrubbed
- 5 kale leaves
- 1 tablespoon olive oil
- 1 carrot
- 2 radishes
- ½ avocado, sliced
- ½ cup ice plant leaves
- handful of cherry tomatoes

Lemon mustard dressing

- 1 tablespoon yellow or dijon mustard
- 2 tablespoons olive oil
- 4 tablespoons lemon juice
- 1 garlic clove, crushed
- pinch of salt and pepper

Preheat the oven to 200°C (400°F).

Wrap the beetroot in aluminium foil and put on a baking tray. Roast for 25–30 minutes or until tender. Let the beetroots cool, then peel off the outer skin. Slice into halves or wedges and put aside.

While the beetroots are cooking, make the dressing by whisking the ingredients in a bowl or jar until combined. Season with a pinch of salt and freshly ground black pepper.

Remove the kale leaves from the stem, discarding the stem. Finely chop the kale greens and put into a large bowl. Add the olive oil and massage the kale to break it down slightly and make it easier to digest.

Cut the carrots into thin matchsticks, then slice the radishes finely into medallions using a sharp knife or mandoline slicer. Wash the ice plant and break into bite-sized pieces. Cut the cherry tomatoes into quarters.

Arrange the cooked beetroot, kale, carrot, radishes, avocado, ice plant and cherry tomatoes in a bowl. Pour over the dressing and serve immediately.

ILLAWARRA PLUM

Podocarpus elatus

No relation to a true plum, this tall evergreen tree is a bit of a botanical oddity. The vivid purple-black fruit is particularly unusual, having a seed that grows externally, at the base of its fleshy stalk. The tree itself, a dense rainforest specimen also known as the brown pine, is also unusual in that it is a pine that bears no cones.

Illawarra plum is native to the subtropical rainforest regions of the east coast of Australia, from New South Wales to Queensland. Unfortunately it has become uncommon in the wild due to extensive logging of its timber, which was highly prized for use in furniture and boat making. The species is planted in great numbers by councils as a shade tree and sold by nurseries for both domestic and commercial purposes.

Chewing the sweet, fleshy stems provided Indigenous Australians with a very valuable source of vitamin C and was also used to treat stomach pains. The ripening fruit served as a cue for hunting: traditional owners would catch the birds and animals that were drawn to the seasonal feast. The strongly resinous and commonly avoided seed was also put to use. They would be roasted and ground, then mixed with water to form a paste that was then consumed.

Illawarra plums are a valuable source of vitamin C, potassium, magnesium and zinc and have an antioxidant content three to five times higher than that of blueberries. They have also been shown to reduce the growth of certain cancer cells, which could lead to the active ingredients being used as an alternative to conventional chemotherapy.

The fleshy fruit of Illawarra plum is similar in texture to a grape, with a sweet and mild pine flavour that has earned it the alternative name of 'plum pine'. The plum-pine flavour of the fruit is delicious in jams, sauces, desserts and drinks or simply eaten raw if you can source them. Illawarra plums are available year-round in frozen form.

ILLAWARRA PLUM FRUIT & NUT CHOCOLATE

MAKES 3 BARS

Illawarra plums have a fresh plum-pine flavour that works really well in these easy-to-make chocolates. We've used silicone break-apart chocolate moulds but partially filled silicone cupcake moulds work just as well.

¼ cup macadamia nuts
1 cup cacao butter
½ cup cacao powder
½ cup maple syrup
1 teaspoon vanilla extract
100 g Illawarra plums, frozen

You'll need 3 break-apart chocolate bar moulds (7 × 15 cm) for this quantity of chocolate.

Start by toasting the macadamia nuts. Put the nuts in a large, dry frying pan and cook on a medium heat for 5 minutes or until the nuts turn slightly golden. Shake the pan often and keep a close eye on it so they don't burn. Remove from the heat and let the macadamias cool on a plate.

Defrost the Illawarra plums, remove the pips and chop the fruit into halves then set aside.

To make the chocolate, bring a small saucepan half filled with water to the boil. Reduce it to a medium simmer and place a large heat-resistant glass bowl on top. The bowl should sit well above the water.

Add the cacao butter to the bowl, stirring until it melts, around 5 minutes. Once the cacao butter has melted stir in the cacao powder, maple syrup and vanilla extract. Gently cook for a couple more minutes or until everything is smooth and well combined. Remove the bowl from the heat and let stand for 15 minutes.

Distribute the chocolate mixture evenly into the moulds. While the chocolate mixture is still soft, gently press the plums and nuts into the chocolate.

Put the moulds in the freezer for at least an hour before removing the bar from the moulds. Store the chocolate in the freezer.

KAKADU PLUM

Terminalia ferdinandiana

One of the most well-known native superfoods, the pale olive-green fruit of the Kakadu plum tree was first brought to the attention of the Australian public in the late 1980s by Les Hiddins, aka 'The Bush Tucker Man', on his television series of the same name. This served as a first introduction for many to the Kakadu plum, but knowledge of this fruit and its impressive medicinal properties has been cherished and passed down by the Indigenous peoples of Australia for thousands of years.

This attractive tree grows to about 10 metres, with an open canopy of symmetrical branches and broad leaves. Native to the tropical woodlands of the north-west and eastern regions of Arnhem Land in the Northern Territory, as well as the east and western Kimberley regions of Western Australia, Kakadu plum trees are still locally abundant in the Top End. While production has mainly come from wild harvest, the rising interest in this super fruit has prompted the establishment of sustainable Kakadu plum plantations within various Aboriginal communities around Australia in an effort to meet the growing demand.

Considered a gift from the Dreamtime, the Kakadu plum has served as more than just a bushfood to the Aboriginal people of Australia. The fruit provided hydration and essential vitamins and the bark of the tree was boiled down and applied topically to treat rashes and burns. The liquid extracted from this process was also drunk to treat inflammation and colds.

As well as being a valuable source of vitamin E, iron, folate, zinc, magnesium, calcium, lutein and powerful antioxidants, Kakadu plum has been found to contain a higher concentration of vitamin C than any other natural source in the world – 100 times the amount found in oranges.

The tart and refreshing flavour of the Kakadu plum is often likened to that of an English gooseberry, with a pleasant aroma of citrus and stewed apple. Due to their acidity, Kakadu plums are great for pickling but work just as well made into a sauce, added to smoothies, or simply eaten raw for a thirst-quenching burst. Kakadu plums are available in powdered, dried and frozen forms and as an essential oil.

KAKADU PLUM & LILLY PILLY SMOOTHIE BOWL

SERVES 2

The lilly pillies add a citrusy note to this sweet smoothie bowl while the Kakadu plum provides a boost of vitamin C. Topped with fresh fruit and some granola for crunch, this is a tasty and nutritious way to start your day.

3 frozen bananas
½ cup lilly pillies, fresh or frozen
1 tablespoon Kakadu plum powder
2 tablespoons chia seeds
2 handfuls baby spinach
½ avocado
½ cup almond milk
fresh fruit, nuts or seeds, to sprinkle (optional)

ALTERNATIVELY
Use your milk preference instead of almond milk.

Put all the ingredients in a blender and blend until smooth. Pour into two bowls and scatter with fresh fruit, nuts or seeds of your choice, if using. Or serve topped with our Passionberry Granola (page 120).

KARKALLA

Carpobrutus rossii

This creeping native groundcover, with its succulent leaves and vibrant pink flowers, is also well known as pigface, due to the pulpy, reddish-pink fruit that is said to resemble the head of its namesake.

Common in coastal environments in southern and western Australia, Tasmania and Victoria, karkalla grows along cliffs and dunes near the ocean, which is what gives this rambling succulent its distinctive, salty flavour. Karkalla is a relative of warrigal greens, and similar species can also be found in southern Africa and South America. Also known as beach bananas, the fleshy leaves of karkalla are grown for commercial purposes in salt water-flooded plots and boxes of composted seaweed across Victoria and South Australia.

Aboriginal people valued karkalla for its mild, salty flavour and the juicy leaves were a plentiful part of their regular diet. The juice of the leaf provided a source of hydration and was also used medicinally as a skin treatment for insect bites and stings. This same liquid was ingested to relieve symptoms of diarrhoea and stomach cramps. The blooming of its beautiful, bright pink flowers also served as an indication that schools of tailor fish were on the move and could be caught in shallow beach areas.

Karkalla has been found to contain significant antioxidant properties as well as antiplatelet and anti-inflammatory qualities. The juice of the stubby leaf continues to be used as a balm for sunburn, insect bites and other skin conditions, in a similar manner to aloe vera. It is also used as a mild astringent and can be gargled to relieve sore throats.

Imbued with a natural briny flavour, the juicy leaves of karkalla are most similar to green beans and make a delicious addition to salads, soups, rice paper rolls and stir-fries. Due to the sustainable commercial production of karkalla, the tender leaves are available fresh year-round but should be used promptly due to their limited shelf life.

KARKALLA NORI ROLLS

MAKES 4

The small green stems of karkalla add a beautiful freshness and salty crunch to these easy-to-make nori rolls.

1 cup quinoa
2 cups water
1 vegetable stock cube
2 tablespoons rice wine vinegar
1 tablespoon mirin
1 packet 18 × 20 cm nori sheets
500 g firm tofu
1 tablespoon coconut oil
1 cup karkalla leaves, stems removed
1 carrot, peeled and sliced into 1 cm strips
1 medium cucumber, sliced into 1 cm strips
1 medium red capsicum, sliced into ½ cm strips
1 avocado, sliced

Wasabi mayonnaise

1 cup raw cashews (soaked for at least 30 minutes)
2 teaspoons wasabi paste
2 teaspoons apple cider vinegar
2 tablespoons lemon juice
1 garlic clove, finely chopped
¼ cup water
salt to taste

NOTE

Bamboo mats are essential for making nori rolls. They can be purchased at supermarkets and are reusable.

Look online for a demonstration if you are unsure about the rolling process.

Rinse the quinoa and combine in a saucepan with the water and stock cube over medium heat. Bring to the boil, then lower the heat and gently simmer for around 15 minutes or until the liquid is absorbed. Transfer the cooked quinoa to a non-reactive bowl, then stir in the vinegar and mirin. Set aside.

To make the wasabi mayonnaise, add all the ingredients to a blender and blend until smooth. Check for its wasabi heat and adjust to desired heat. Transfer to a small bowl.

While you're preparing the tofu, heat the oil in a frying pan.

Slice the tofu into 1 cm thick slabs and add to the pan. Cook over a medium heat until the tofu is golden on both sides. Let cool and cut into 1 cm strips.

To assemble the rolls, place a nori sheet, shiny side down, onto a bamboo mat. Spoon on the quinoa – and flatten it out – so that the lower three quarters of the sheet is evenly covered. Leave the top quarter of the sheet uncovered. Arrange the vegetables and tofu neatly – everything lengthways – on top of the quinoa. Be careful not to overload the wrapper as this will make rolling difficult. Then drizzle over about 1 teaspoon of the wasabi mayonnaise.

Start to gently and firmly roll, using the edge of the bamboo mat to guide you. Stop at the uncovered section of the nori sheet and gently brush it with water. Finish rolling up the rest of the sheet, making sure everything has been tightly rolled and sealed. Repeat for the remaining sheets.

Cut each roll into 2-3 cm pieces using a sharp straight-edge knife. You'll get a much cleaner cut if the knife is super sharp and dampened with water, but do take care.

Serve with tamari or soy sauce and extra wasabi mayonnaise.

Nori rolls are best prepared fresh and served immediately.

KUTJERA

Solanum centrale

Although there are some 100 species of wild tomatoes native to outback Australia, only six are known to be safe for consumption. One such species is kutjera, also known as the desert raisin – a small globular fruit borne by a tough desert shrub. The fruit begins green, turns yellow when fully ripe and dries to a gnarled reddish brown.

Kutjera is found in arid desert areas of the Northern Territory, South Australia and Western Australia and grows on a compact bush, about 1 metre high. Until recently it was mostly sourced from the wild, but it is now also grown commercially in Aboriginal communities in South Australia and the Northern Territory.

Bush tomatoes have been an important bushfood staple in the diets of Indigenous Australians for thousands of years. The fruits of the plant would be left to sun-dry on the bush before being eaten and were thought to help boost immunity as well as provide energy in an easy-to-pick and portable form. The roots of the plant were also used as a natural remedy for toothaches when baked in ash, peeled and applied to painful teeth.

These small fruits are one of the only native bushfoods to contain selenium, a trace mineral and powerful antioxidant that helps to prevent oxidative damage to the body. Kutjera fruit is also an excellent source of folate, magnesium, iron, potassium, zinc and vitamins C and E.

Kutjera has an intense, tangy flavour with a hint of sweetness not dissimilar to regular sun-dried tomatoes. It works best in savoury dishes and particularly complements tomato-based recipes such as soups, pasta sauces and salsas. Kutjera can also be ground and blended with other bush spices and nuts to make a unique and delicious dukkah. Available in dried or powdered form, it is said that dried kutjera can keep for up to two years.

KUTJERA PASTA

SERVES 3-4

The kutjera adds a rich depth to this comforting pasta sauce and, like semi-dried tomatoes, a little goes a long way.

- 1 tablespoon olive oil
- 1 onion, diced
- 2 garlic cloves, crushed
- 1 long red chilli, finely diced (more or less, depending on heat preference)
- 2 carrots, chopped
- 1 zucchini, chopped
- 1 red capsicum, chopped
- 6 kutjera, diced
- 2 × 400 g tinned crushed tomatoes
- 2 × 400 g tinned chickpeas, rinsed and drained
- 1 tablespoon tomato paste
- 1 vegetable stock cube, crumbled
- 1 teaspoon dried oregano
- 1 teaspoon dried native thyme
- ½ teaspoon ground fennel
- ½ teaspoon dried cinnamon myrtle
- ½ teaspoon dried native basil
- ¼ teaspoon mountain pepper leaf
- 1 bay leaf
- fresh basil, to serve
- packet of buckwheat pasta

Heat the olive oil in a heavy-based saucepan over medium heat. Sauté the onion, cooking for 5 minutes until translucent, then add the garlic and chilli and cook for a further minute, until fragrant. Stir in the carrots, zucchini and capsicum and cook for 5 minutes until softened.

Add all remaining ingredients to the vegetable base, mixing well. Reduce heat to a low simmer and cook for 20 minutes, stirring frequently, until the sauce has thickened. Add a splash of water if sauce is too thick. Season to taste.

Cook the buckwheat pasta as per the packet instructions, until al dente. Serve immediately with kutjera sauce. Garnish with fresh basil leaves, if using.

LEMON ASPEN

Acronychia acidula

The beautiful pale-yellow fruit of this small rainforest tree earned the species name *acidula* – 'slightly acid' in Latin – for its deliciously sharp citrus aroma and flavour, characteristic of the common lemon. The intense flavour of lemon aspen sees it used in a growing range of gourmet products such as juices, jellies and dressings.

Endemic to the rainforests and tablelands of tropical north Queensland, lemon aspen is one of around 20 species of *Acronychia* native to Australia and one of 44 species worldwide. Though not widely cultivated, lemon aspen is grown in some small-scale orchards along the east coast of Australia with the involvement of local Aboriginal communities.

The Indigenous peoples of Australia traditionally enjoyed the fruits of the lemon aspen picked straight from the tree for their fresh, zesty flavour. They also extracted the juice by crushing the fruit, drinking it to boost immunity and soothe sore throats. It also served as a natural antiseptic and was applied to sores and boils.

Packed with antioxidants and a rich source of vitamins B and C, the fruit of the lemon aspen also contains compounds known to encourage skin regeneration, which has made it a widely used ingredient in anti-aging and skin repair products. Lemon aspen is also a valuable source of folate, zinc, iron, magnesium, calcium, manganese, potassium and phosphorus.

Lemon aspen works well in place of regular lemons, although not a lot of the fruit is needed due to its intensity. Lemon aspen makes delicious jams, fruit curds, dessert sauces and tarts and is available in fresh, frozen and juice form. The fresh fruit will keep in the fridge for up to three weeks, while the frozen form will keep for up to two years.

LEMON ASPEN SLICE

MAKES 10

This is one of Tom's favourite childhood treats, revised to make use of the delicious, tangy fruits of the lemon aspen.

Base

1 cup macadamia nuts
1 cup desiccated coconut
½ cup dates, pitted
1 tablespoon grated lemon zest

Filling

1 cup raw cashews (soaked for at least 30 minutes)
1 cup lemon aspen, frozen
½ cup desiccated coconut
¼ cup lemon juice
¼ cup maple syrup
¼ cup coconut oil
1 tablespoon grated lemon zest, plus extra to garnish

Line a 1 litre loaf pan (10 × 20 cm) with baking paper.

To make the base, combine the macadamia nuts, coconut, dates and lemon zest in a blender and blitz until the mixture forms a crumbly paste. Add this mixture to the loaf pan, spread it out evenly and press down firmly with the back of a spoon. Pop the base in the freezer while you make the filling.

To make the filling, combine all the ingredients in a blender and pulse until smooth. Pour the filling over the crust and spread evenly. Freeze for 4 hours to set.

Cut the slice into pieces. Let slice sit for 15–20 minutes before serving. Top with freshly grated lemon zest.

LEMON MYRTLE

Backhousia citriodora

Revered as the queen of the lemon herbs and undoubtedly one of the most well-known and widely used Australian bush superfoods, this intensely fragrant plant is easily identified by its beautiful citrus aroma and clusters of feathery, white flowers.

This medium-sized aromatic shrub naturally occurs in the wet coastal rainforest areas of northern New South Wales and southern Queensland. It is one of the most cultivated Australian native bushfoods, with more than 15,000 lemon myrtle trees planted in Victoria, New South Wales and Queensland in an attempt to meet the growing commercial demand for this herb.

Now widely used in the culinary and cosmetic worlds, Indigenous Australians were the first to recognise the nutritional and healing benefits of this valuable native plant. Chewing on the leaves of the lemon myrtle provided a boost of vitamins and minerals while the antibacterial properties within helped ward off disease and infection. The glossy green leaves would also be ground into a paste and applied to sores and other skin afflictions.

Lemon myrtle is the highest known natural source of plant citral – a fragrant, naturally occurring liquid with powerful anti-inflammatory and antimicrobial qualities – making it a much sought after ingredient in health products. Lemon myrtle is also extremely high in calcium and antioxidants and a valuable source of magnesium, vitamin E and lutein.

The intense lemon-lime flavour and aroma of lemon myrtle makes it a great addition to curries, sauce, and dessert dishes, and is used in much the same way as lemon zest, kaffir lime or lemongrass. The leaves can also be used to make a fragrant, relaxing herbal tea when infused in hot or cold water. Lemon myrtle is widely available fresh, dried or in ground form and as an essential oil.

LEMON MYRTLE & DILL CASHEW CHEESE

MAKES 2 CUPS

The zest of the lemon myrtle in this cashew cheese pairs well with the dill and creates a delicious spread that works as a dip or on sandwiches. Team it with our Sandalwood Nut & Seed Crackers (page 152).

- 2 cups raw cashews (soaked for at least 30 minutes)
- 2 garlic cloves, finely chopped
- 1 teaspoon dried lemon myrtle
- 2 tablespoons nutritional yeast
- 1 teaspoon miso paste
- 2 tablespoons lemon juice
- 1 teaspoon apple cider vinegar
- salt and pepper
- 2 tablespoons fresh dill, finely chopped, plus extra for garnish

Add all the ingredients, except the dill, to a blender and pulse until smooth. Stir in the chopped dill. Check the seasoning.

Transfer the cashew cheese to a resealable container or sterilised jar and top with additional chopped dill. This cheese will last up to a week stored in the fridge.

NATIVE LEMONGRASS

Cymbopogon ambiguus

This widespread native grass – with its green foliage and stems and upright silver seed heads – is becoming a common sight in contemporary Australian gardens, a favourite for its beautiful aroma, adaptability and low maintenance requirements.

Tolerant of frost and extreme drought conditions, this strappy grass grows prolifically in hot, arid regions of Australia, particularly in northern South Australia, but is also found dispersed throughout northern Queensland, the Northern Territory, New South Wales and Western Australia. Due to its popularity as an ornamental, native lemongrass is now readily available from native plant nurseries.

An important bush medicine to the Aboriginal people of central Australia, native lemongrass has long been utilised to treat a wide range of ailments. Respiratory difficulties were relieved by crushing and sniffing the stems, while an infusion of the crushed roots and stems was also used to soothe muscular cramps, headaches and diarrhoea. That same concoction was also applied topically to treat sores, scabies and other skin ailments.

Results of a recent five-year study found that native lemongrass was equally as effective as aspirin in relieving headaches and migraines. This is due to a bioactive compound called eugenol, also found in cloves, that contains powerful antioxidant, anti-inflammatory, antifungal and antiseptic properties. It has been used commercially in dentistry, skin care products and veterinary medications.

A relative of the common tropical lemongrass used in Asian cooking, *Cymbopogon citratus*, native lemongrass has a similar beautiful citric aroma and refreshing lemon-lime flavour and can be used in much the same way in soups, curries and other coconut-based dishes. A calming and digestive tea can also be made by infusing a handful of native lemongrass stems in hot water for 3–5 minutes and adding sweetener if desired. Native lemongrass is available dried and in various herbal tea blends.

NATIVE LEMONGRASS PUMPKIN SOUP

SERVES 4

This combination of roasted pumpkin and native lemongrass makes for a delicious, comforting soup, perfect for the colder months.

Pumpkin soup

8 cups butternut and kent pumpkin
6 garlic cloves
3 teaspoons dried native lemongrass, chopped
1 teaspoon freshly grated nutmeg
4 tablespoons coconut oil
salt and pepper
2 onions, diced
4 cups vegetable stock
¼ cup toasted pepitas, to serve
handful of roughly chopped coriander leaves, to serve
1 red chilli, sliced, to serve (optional)

Jalapeño & coriander cashew cream

2 jalapeños, chopped
1 tablespoon chopped coriander
1 cup raw cashews (soaked for at least 30 minutes)
1 garlic clove
1 teaspoon apple cider vinegar
½ cup water
salt and pepper

Preheat the oven to 200°C (400°F) and line two large baking trays with baking paper.

Peel and remove the seeds from the pumpkin and chop into 2–3 cm cubes. Transfer to a large mixing bowl together with the garlic, native lemongrass, nutmeg, 3 tablespoons of coconut oil and a good pinch of salt and freshly ground black pepper. Mix until the pumpkin is well coated, then arrange in a single layer on the baking trays. Bake for 1 hour or until the pumpkin is soft, turning the pieces and turning trays after 30 minutes.

Meanwhile, make the jalapeño and coriander cashew cream by combining all the ingredients in a blender and mixing until smooth.

Heat the remaining coconut oil in a large stockpot over a low-medium heat. Sauté the onion for 5 minutes or until translucent. Add the roasted pumpkin and vegetable stock and bring to the boil, then simmer for 15 minutes. Add the mixture to a blender in batches, or use a hand-held blender, and blitz until smooth. Check the seasoning.

Ladle the hot soup into bowls and dollop the jalapeño cream on top. Finish with toasted pepitas, coriander and chilli, if using.

LILLY PILLY

Syzygium smithii

It may come as a surprise to some that the plentiful reddish-pink to white berry-like fruit of this widely used hedging plant is also one of Australia's most potent superfoods. While the name lilly pilly once applied to just one species, it now refers to over 50 related varieties, all with edible fruit.

These hardy rainforest trees occur naturally in coastal rainforests along the east coast of Australia, from Queensland to Victoria, and have a lush, bushy habit, with attractive pink new growth. The ripe fruit is much loved by birds and possums. First introduced into cultivation at the Royal Botanic Gardens in England by botanist and naturalist Sir Joseph Banks in 1790, many forms of lilly pilly have since been chosen for commercial cultivation across Australia.

Long utilised by the Aboriginal peoples of the east coast of Australia, the daguba fruit or 'medicine berries' as they came to be known, have been a bushfood dietary staple, eaten raw as a sweet treat and as a valuable source of essential vitamins and minerals.

Bursting with antioxidants and amino acids, the refreshing fruits of the lilly pilly are rich in vitamins A, C and E, promoting healthy bone growth, skin regeneration, good eye health and boosting the immune system. It is also interesting to note that just 100g of lilly pilly fruit contains 50% of the recommended daily intake of folate.

The fruit of the lilly pilly has a sweet fragrance and a slightly tart flavour not unlike that of a cranberry or crab apple, and works well when made into a jam, marinade or sauce, or added to smoothies. Lilly pillies can be eaten fresh and will keep for up to two weeks after being picked; otherwise they can be frozen for later use. They are readily available frozen year-round.

LILLY PILLY & BANANA SWIRL ICE CREAMS

MAKES 7-8

Lilly pilly and banana are a winning flavour combination and these sweet, creamy ice creams are no exception. You will need popsicle moulds and sticks for this easy-to-make treat.

Lilly pilly mixture

1 cup lilly pillies, fresh or frozen, deseeded

½ cup almond milk

1 tablespoon maple syrup

Banana mixture

4 frozen bananas

1 cup raw cashews (soaked for at least 30 minutes)

2 cups almond milk

2 tablespoons maple syrup

1 teaspoon vanilla extract

Add the lilly pillies to a blender and blend until smooth. Pour the puree into a bowl and set aside.

Combine the frozen bananas, cashews, almond milk, maple syrup and vanilla extract in a blender and process until smooth. Pour into a large mixing bowl.

Using a spoon, alternate filling up the popsicle moulds with the two mixtures until the moulds are full. Aim for 4 or 5 layers in each. Push in the popsicle sticks and jiggle them a little to achieve a swirl effect.

Freeze for at least 6 hours to get a good solid set.

ALTERNATIVELY

Use your milk preference instead of almond milk.

NOTE

Paper cups make great ice-cream moulds as well. Just dip them into warm water to help remove the ice creams. We bought our popsicle sticks from an art and craft shop.

MACADAMIA NUT

Macadamia integrifolia (smooth shell)
Tetraphylla (rough shell)

Named after Dr John Macadam, a Scottish-Australian chemist, politician and once Honorary Secretary of the Royal Society of Victoria, the creamy nut of the macadamia tree possesses one of the hardest nut shells in the world and is easily one of Australia's top horticultural exports.

These attractive trees, which can grow up to 20 metres in the wild, are native to the subtropical rainforests of New South Wales and south-east Queensland. From the first commercial orchard planted in the 1880s, there are now some 850 growers in Australia, yielding over 40,000 tonnes of nuts per year, most of which are exported. Hybrid cultivars of both species are commercially available. Macadamia trees have since been naturalised into various other parts of the world including Hawaii, South Africa, Brazil and Israel where the nuts are now commercially produced.

Macadamia nuts were prized for their high energy and fat content by Indigenous Australians, who developed a clever method of cracking the hard shells to obtain the sweet nut within. They secured the macadamia on an indented stone base with a flat stone placed on top, then used a larger stone as a hammer. The oil of the nut was also used as a binder with clay and ochre to make body paint.

Oil extracted from the macadamia nut is widely regarded as one of the healthiest edible oils in the world, boasting an impressively low saturated fat content and rich in high-quality monounsaturated fat. Macadamia nuts are also high in dietary fibre, essential vitamins and minerals – particularly thiamin, manganese and copper – and are antioxidant-rich and cholesterol-free.

These sweet, velvety nuts are similar to Brazil nuts and likewise are delicious eaten raw, plain roasted or in savoury and sweet dishes. Macadamia nuts are particularly suited to chocolates, salads, nut butters and pesto recipes and are available year-round from most supermarkets, in a variety of forms including raw and roasted. Dried macadamia nuts will keep for up to nine months, but can also be frozen for up to two years.

BLACK BEAN & MACADAMIA NUT BROWNIES

MAKES 8–10

You may be apprehensive about using black beans as the base of a dessert recipe, we were too. The result, however, is a moist, decadent brownie with absolutely no bean taste.

Brownies

2 tablespoons ground chia seeds
6 tablespoons water
400 g tinned black beans
4 tablespoons cacao powder
2 teaspoons ground wattleseed
1 teaspoon vanilla extract
3 tablespoons coconut oil
½ cup rice malt syrup
½ teaspoon dried cinnamon myrtle
1 teaspoon gluten-free baking powder
1 teaspoon gluten-free baking soda
1 handful raw macadamia nuts, roughly chopped
strawberries or blueberries, to serve (optional)

Macadamia cream

1 cup raw macadamias (soaked for at least 30 minutes)
½ teaspoon vanilla extract
1 teaspoon ground wattleseed
2 tablespoons maple syrup
¼ cup water

Preheat the oven to 175°C (340°F) and line an oiled 12 × 27 cm baking tin with baking paper.

Combine the ground chia with the water, stir and let sit for 15 minutes.

Rinse and drain the black beans well. Add the beans to a blender along with the chia mixture and all other ingredients except the chopped macadamia nuts. Blend until smooth.

Pour the brownie mixture into the baking tin and top with the chopped nuts. Bake for 25–30 minutes or until the sides begin to rise.

Meanwhile, make the macadamia cream by putting all the ingredients into a blender and blending until smooth.

Leave the brownies to cool completely in the tin, then put in the fridge for at least 1 hour to set. When nicely chilled, and still in the tin, cut the brownies into squares. Carefully lift out.

Serve with a dollop of macadamia cream and fresh berries, if using.

MOUNTAIN PEPPER

Tasmannia lanceolata

Famed for its earthy, spicy heat, the purple-black, berry-like fruit of the mountain pepper, sometimes referred to as Tasmanian pepper, is an increasingly popular substitute for regular pepper.

Favouring cool-wet climates, the mountain pepper is an attractive glossy leaved shrub growing in high-country forests of south-east Australia, from the Blue Mountains of New South Wales to Tasmania. Both the berries and leaves of the mountain pepper can be used and are now commercially grown in cooler parts of Australia. Mountain pepper berries are exported to Japan to add flavour to wasabi.

Not just a contemporary spice, mountain pepper has been used by Indigenous Australians as a bush medicine for centuries. The fresh berries would be crushed and mixed with water to make an effective, but slightly stinging, antibacterial paste that would be applied to infected gums or teeth as well as rashes and other skin abrasions. The bark was also boiled into a liquid tonic to aid digestion and stimulate appetite.

Known also for their anti-inflammatory properties, mountain pepper berries have long been used in traditional medicine to relieve arthritis and other joint conditions. The deep black berries are a rich source of folate, zinc, magnesium, manganese and antioxidants. Perhaps less well known is that the leaves themselves are an antioxidant powerhouse. They contain an estimated three times the amount of antioxidants found in blueberries and have high levels of folate, zinc, magnesium, calcium, iron, lutein and vitamins A and E.

Mountain pepper berries taste uniquely spicy with herbal dimensions and can be used in much the same way as conventional pepper. They are readily available in dried form, whole or ground. The aromatic pepper leaves have a subtler flavour and can be used fresh (seasonally available) or dried and make a great addition to curries and stews.

MOUNTAIN PEPPER GOLDEN LATTE

MAKES 15

Golden lattes are one of the most delicious ways to benefit from the potent antioxidant and anti-inflammatory effects of turmeric. This calming brew is perfect for evenings as the reishi mushroom aids relaxation.

- 1 teaspoon dried mountain pepper berries
- ¼ teaspoon ground black pepper
- 5 tablespoons ground turmeric
- 1 teaspoon ground cinnamon
- 1 teaspoon ground ginger
- ½ teaspoon ground cardamom
- 1 teaspoon natural vanilla powder
- 1-2 teaspoons reishi powder (optional)
- almond milk

ALTERNATIVELY

Use your milk preference instead of almond milk.

Add all the dry ingredients to a blender and blend into a fine powder. This mixture will keep for several months when stored in an airtight container in a cool, dark place.

To make one golden latte, combine 1 teaspoon of golden latte mixture with 1 cup of almond milk in a small saucepan. Heat on a low heat until warm, stirring frequently. Serve as is or add your sweetener of choice, topped with additional ground cinnamon.

NOTE

Vanilla extract can replace the vanilla powder; just add ¼ teaspoon of vanilla extract for each cup of milk when heating.

MUNTRY

Kunzea pomifera

One of Australia's oldest bushfoods and one of the first Australian native plants to have been introduced into cultivation in Britain, the greenish-red fruits of this low-growing plant are also known as emu apples or crab apples due to their spicy apple flavour and resemblance to tiny crab apples. They are also referred to as native cranberries.

This hardy native groundcover favours the coastal environments of south-east South Australia, Kangaroo Island and western Victoria, but can also be found growing inland. Muntry plants are commercially grown for their fruit in a number of plantations in South Australia as well as several local Aboriginal communities, with some 5000 plants currently growing. They are also sold by native plant nurseries as an ornamental groundcover.

Feasted on in the summer months and dried and stored for the winter months, muntry fruit played a significant role in the diets of the Ngarrindjeri people of the Coorong in south-east South Australia with the fruit commonly ground into a paste and shaped into cakes. When left in the sun to dry, these cakes would keep for several months and were often used in trading with other clans.

Muntries are high in vitamin C and contain four times the amount of antioxidants found in blueberries as well as beneficial antiviral and antibacterial properties. Studies have also found that muntries inhibit the growth and proliferation of cancer cells. The fruit contains natural waxes that provide skin nourishment, which has made them a much-desired ingredient in skin care and beauty products.

Muntries have an aroma of spiced fruit and a sweet, spicy apple flavour and may be used in place of apples in cooking. The fresh fruit is delicious eaten raw, added to fruit salads or cooked into jams, pies or crumbles and also works in savoury dishes such as chutneys and sauces. Muntries are available fresh in late summer, but are otherwise available frozen or dried year-round.

JACKFRUIT TACOS WITH MUNTRY COLESLAW

SERVES 4-6

Jackfruit is a surprising but totally successful substitute for pulled pork in this dish. The apple-like flavour of the muntries in the coleslaw is complementary, while the cashew mayonnaise counteracts the spiciness. Adjust the cayenne and jalapeño amounts to suit your heat preference.

2 × 565 g tinned young jackfruit in brine
2 tablespoons olive oil
1 large onion, finely chopped
5 garlic cloves, chopped
1 tablespoon maple syrup
1 tablespoon apple cider vinegar
3 tablespoons tamari or soy sauce
2 teaspoons ground cumin
2 teaspoons sweet paprika
1 teaspoon ground coriander
1 teaspoon dried cinnamon myrtle
1 teaspoon mustard powder
½ teaspoon cayenne pepper
1 teaspoon dried oregano
1 bay leaf
1 or ½ jalapeño chilli, deseeded
2 cups vegetable stock

Muntry coleslaw

½ cup muntries, whole frozen
1 cup raw cashews (soaked for at least 30 minutes)
1 tablespoon lemon juice
½ teaspoon mustard powder
½ teaspoon apple cider vinegar
½ teaspoon maple syrup
¾ cup water
salt and pepper to taste
½ cabbage, finely shredded
2 carrots, grated
2 spring onions (scallions), finely chopped, plus extra to garnish
½ teaspoon celery salt

2 packets small corn tortillas, to serve
chopped avocado, to serve

Drain and rinse the jackfruit in a colander, then place in a large bowl. Pull apart the jackfruit flesh from the harder core with your hands or a fork. Set aside.

Heat the oil in a large stockpot over medium heat. Add the onion and sauté for 5 minutes or until translucent. Then add the garlic and cook for a further minute.

Transfer the shredded jackfruit and the rest of the ingredients to the stockpot and simmer, uncovered, for 40-45 minutes or until most of the liquid has evaporated.

While the jackfruit is cooking, make the mayonnaise for the coleslaw. Combine the muntries, cashews, lemon juice, mustard powder, vinegar, maple syrup, water, salt and pepper in a blender and pulse until smooth. Check the seasoning.

Combine the coleslaw vegetables in a large bowl with the celery salt. Fold through the muntry mayonnaise, tossing until everything is well combined.

To serve, heat the tortillas in a large dry frying pan on a medium heat for 15-30 seconds on each side. We like to bend them a little to stand them up, but you can easily just fold them in half. Do this while they're still hot.

Fill the centre of each tortilla with a generous quantity of the hot jackfruit, then top with some of the muntry coleslaw. Serve with avocado and chopped spring onions.

NOTE

Young jackfruit is readily available in most Asian supermarkets. Make sure to check that it is in brine, as it is also available in syrup.

MUNYEROO

Portulaca oleracea

This widely celebrated tender succulent, also known as purslane in many parts of the world, earned the nickname 'pigweed' in Australia due to its namesake's particular fondness for it. It has tender, trailing stems and paddle-shaped leaves and grows in a compact prostrate form. A forager's dream, munyeroo is commonly available, low-growing and easy to pick.

Though considered a weed in some parts of the world, munyeroo is appreciated for its culinary uses throughout Europe, the Middle East, parts of Asia and Mexico, and has been a valued food source for hundreds, even thousands, of years. In Australia, munyeroo is widespread, growing all over the mainland, particularly favouring the sandy plains and riverbanks of inland Australia. While commonly and easily harvested from the wild, munyeroo is also grown in nurseries to supply the ever-growing bushfood industry.

Traditionally, it was the seeds of munyeroo that were most valued by Indigenous Australians. The tiny, nutrient-dense black seeds would be collected, mashed into a flour and mixed with water to form a paste. This paste could be eaten raw, but was more commonly cooked in hot ashes to make seed cakes rich in protein, iron and essential fats.

While the seeds alone well and truly qualify munyeroo as a native superfood, the plant itself boasts incredible nutritional qualities including an omega-3 content unmatched by any other leafy vegetable. Rich in vitamins A, B, C and E and a valuable source of calcium, magnesium and potassium, munyeroo is also a natural diuretic, meaning it may also help to lower blood pressure.

The mild-flavoured munyeroo leaves are commonly used as a substitute for spinach, with the succulent stems used in a similar way to asparagus. Munyeroo can be added to salads, stir-fries, or simply sautéed with some garlic and tamari. If you're able to acquire them, the linseed-like seeds make a great addition to breads and biscuits. Munyeroo is available fresh year-round.

MUNYEROO SOBA NOODLES WITH WASABI DRESSING

SERVES 3-4

Just-blanched munyeroo - leaves and stems - is a delicious addition to this noodle salad that pairs well with the raw green vegetables. It makes for a tasty summer lunch dish or light dinner.

Soba noodle salad

2 handfuls munyeroo, fresh whole

1 packet buckwheat soba noodles

1 cup snow peas, trimmed and chopped

1 cup sugar snap peas, trimmed and chopped

2 spring onions, sliced, to garnish

lemon wedges, to garnish (optional)

Wasabi dressing

2 teaspoons wasabi paste (more or less, depending on heat preference)

1 cup raw cashews (soaked for at least 30 minutes)

1 garlic clove, finely chopped

2 teaspoons apple cider vinegar

2 tablespoons lemon juice

½ cup water

salt to taste

Bring a medium-sized saucepan of water to the boil and blanch the munyeroo for 1 minute. Remove and add to a bowl of cold water to refresh. Drain thoroughly.

Return the water to the boil and cook the soba noodles as per the packet instructions.

To make the wasabi dressing, add all the ingredients to a blender and blend until smooth. Check the seasoning and adjust if necessary.

To assemble the salad, serve the soba noodles with the munyeroo, snow peas and sugar snap peas, then top with the wasabi dressing. Garnish with spring onion and a wedge of lemon, if using.

PASSIONBERRY

Solanum cleistogamum

This sweet member of the native bush tomato family was once widespread in outback Australia thanks to the indigenous wildlife that would eat the aromatic, pale yellow fruit and scatter the undigested seeds via their droppings. In more recent times, this prickly native shrub suffered such overgrazing by stock and feral animals that it was feared extinct.

Occurring naturally in isolated patches of gravelly terrain, predominantly in desert regions of the Northern Territory and Western Australia, this low-spreading shrub has since been introduced into small-scale cultivation in Aboriginal communities with great results. Due to the fruit's very limited shelf life, it is harvested and then dried or frozen to avoid spoilage.

These sweet fruits have long been a source of nutrition and hydration for Indigenous Australians, with uses beyond that of solely a bushfood. As with its relative *S. centrale*, the roots of the passionberry were also used to treat toothache by roasting and peeling the roots and applying them to affected teeth or gums. It is also thought to have been used as a natural contraceptive due to steroids contained in the plants; research is now being undertaken into the potential use of the plant's steroids in the manufacture of commercial contraceptives.

As with other varieties of native bush tomato, the light yellow fruits of the passionberry are exceptionally high in vitamin C and antioxidants including selenium and other essential nutrients such as potassium, folate, iron, zinc, magnesium and calcium.

The raisin-like passionberry fruits are surprisingly sweet and aromatic, with flavours of banana and caramel. They make a delicious dessert sauce or addition to muesli, smoothies and muffins, or can be gently stewed as a compote. It should be noted that when cooking with passionberries, care should be taken to not overcook the fruits as they will take on an unpleasant burnt flavour. Passionberries are available dried and frozen year-round.

PASSIONBERRY GRANOLA

SERVES 4

This makes for a great breakfast served with coconut yoghurt and fresh berries. The passionberries have a comforting banana bread-like flavour that is enhanced by the cinnamon in this granola.

½ cup macadamia nuts, chopped
½ cup raw almonds, chopped
4 tablespoons maple syrup
½ cup chia seeds
2 cups quinoa flakes
4 tablespoons coconut oil
1 teaspoon vanilla extract
1 tablespoon rice malt syrup
2 teaspoons ground cinnamon
1 cup dried passionberries
coconut yoghurt or your milk preference, to serve
fresh berries (optional)

Preheat the oven to 175°C (340°F). Line a large baking tray with baking paper.

Combine the macadamia nuts, almonds, maple syrup, chia seeds, quinoa flakes, coconut oil, vanilla extract, rice malt syrup and ground cinnamon in a large bowl and mix thoroughly until everything is well coated.

Transfer the granola mixture to the lined baking tray and spread out evenly. Bake for 25 minutes, shaking and turning once. Remove tray from the oven and leave to cool completely on a wire rack.

Pour the granola into a large mixing bowl and stir through the passionberries. Serve with yoghurt or your milk preference and fresh berries, if using.

The granola will keep in a large sealed jar for up to a month.

PEPPERMINT GUM

Eucalyptus dives

One of the most well known of Australia's eucalypts, the peppermint gum, also known as the broad-leaved peppermint, is widely planted both at home and abroad for its pendulous, shade-giving canopy and beautiful, mint-scented foliage.

Native to the dry woodlands and forests of south-eastern Australia, the peppermint gum, along with more than 200 other species of eucalypts, has been introduced to many other parts of the world, such as California and Sri Lanka. This variety is now widely commercially grown.

Favoured by Indigenous Australians not only for its fresh aroma and delicious flavour, the leaves of the peppermint gum also proved a useful remedy for gastrointestinal symptoms when mixed with water and drunk. The aromatic smoke of burning peppermint gum leaves was used to relieve fever symptoms and, as is the case with many other varieties of eucalypt, the roots of the peppermint gum could also be tapped for water in times of need.

Today the leaves of the peppermint gum are commonly used for the production of eucalyptus oil, an essential oil well known for its wide-ranging health benefits. The antiseptic, decongestant, anti-inflammatory and antimicrobial properties of eucalyptus oil are widely researched and reported, and today the oil is used in a myriad of applications.

Used as a flavouring in billy tea since colonial times, peppermint gum leaves have a fresh peppermint flavour and aroma with eucalyptus undertones that works particularly well in sweet recipes such as cakes and chocolates. It also makes a delicious, relaxing herbal tea when brewed in hot water for 2–3 minutes. Peppermint gum leaves are available dried year-round and can be found in various herbal tea blends.

PEPPERMINT GUM, CACAO & DATE BLISS BALLS

MAKES 15-20

These super-charged bliss balls with maca and chaga powders and dates are the perfect pick-me-up for those afternoon lulls in energy.

- 2 cups almond meal
- 1 cup raw cashews (soaked for at least 30 minutes)
- 2 tablespoons cacao powder
- 12 dates, pitted
- 1 tablespoon chia seeds
- 1 tablespoon maca powder
- ½–1 teaspoon chaga powder
- 1 teaspoon dried peppermint gum
- 1 teaspoon dried river mint
- ½ teaspoon vanilla extract
- 2 teaspoons coconut oil, melted
- 1 teaspoon Kakadu plum powder (optional)
- ½ cup crushed macadamia nuts, almonds or dessicated coconut to coat (optional)

Put all the ingredients in a blender and mix until combined to a dough-like consistency.

Using your hands, roll the mixture into small balls, about the size of a walnut, then coat in crushed macadamia nuts, almonds or dessicated coconut if desired.

Chill the balls for at least 3 hours to set. These will keep for several weeks if stored in an airtight container in the fridge.

ALTERNATIVELY
Fresh mint leaves can be used instead of river mint.

QUANDONG

Santalum acuminatum

Considered a godsend by many a weary outback traveller, the fruit of the quandong tree – also known as the desert peach – is an attractive, bright scarlet fruit with many beneficial uses.

Quandongs are widely dispersed throughout the arid inland and coastal regions of southern Australia including Western Australia, South Australia, Northern Territory, Victoria and New South Wales, with remnant communities in remote areas. The quandong grows to a shrubby tree and is a relative of the sandalwood. It has now been successfully commercially cultivated, with over 40,000 trees growing in plantations.

Traditionally used to ward off sickness due to the fruit's high concentration of vitamin C, Aboriginal people also utilised the kernel and leaves of the quandong, crushing them and mixing them with saliva to use as a topical treatment for skin ailments. The root was also ground and boiled into a tea that was drunk to treat inflammation and soothe joint pain. No part of the quandong was wasted: the juicy flesh of the fruit was considered a suitable substitute for meat and the decorative round seed was used to make necklaces and game pieces.

While the magnesium, iron, zinc and antioxidant content of the quandong flesh is more than enough to justify its superfood status, the kernel of the fruit, which contains complex oils and impressive antibacterial and anti-inflammatory properties, is a superfood in its own right. Quandongs are also a fantastic source of vitamins, containing twice the amount of vitamin C found in oranges.

Sweet and slightly sour, quandongs are often compared to an apricot. The fruit flesh makes a fantastic jam, relish or dessert sauce. Quandongs are most commonly sourced frozen or dried, with the seed already removed. In dried form they have an exceptionally long shelf life. The commercial marketability of the edible and nutrient-dense kernel, however, has yet to be realised.

QUANDONG SYRUP PANCAKES

MAKES 15

These fluffy pancakes are a terrific base for most fruit sauces and purees. This sweet and tangy quandong syrup is spot on with them – if you've got any left over, use it as a topping on coconut yoghurt or as a cocktail base.

Quandong syrup

½ cup dried quandongs, soaked
½ cup maple syrup
1 tablespoon lemon juice

Pancakes

½ cup dried quandongs, soaked
2 cups almond milk
2 cups buckwheat flour
1 cup almond flour
2 bananas, mashed
2 teaspoons ground wattleseed
2–4 tablespoons maple syrup
1 teaspoon cinnamon
1 teaspoon vanilla extract
1 teaspoon gluten-free baking powder
coconut oil for frying
sliced banana and blueberrries, to serve

ALTERNATIVELY

Use your milk preference instead of almond milk.

Soak the quandongs for both the syrup and the pancakes in a large bowl of warm water for 30 minutes. Drain and set aside.

To make the syrup, add ½ a cup of the soaked quandongs to a blender and blitz until smooth. Combine the pureed quandongs, maple syrup and lemon juice in a small saucepan and simmer on a low heat for 10 minutes, stirring frequently.

To make the pancakes, chop up the remaining ½ cup of soaked quandongs and combine with all of the pancake ingredients in a large mixing bowl. Mix the batter well until smooth.

Heat a large frying pan over a low-medium heat with enough coconut oil to coat the pan. It does pay to have the pan good and hot before the first pancake is made. For each pancake, add roughly 3 tablespoons of the batter to the pan and cook for a couple of minutes on each side or until golden. Cook in batches and cover with aluminium foil to keep them warm. Add more coconut oil if the pan starts to look dry.

Serve the pancakes with the quandong syrup and fresh fruit.

RIBERRY

Syzygium luehmannii

Of the same family and genus as the common lilly pilly, the riberry bears spectacular masses of pink berry-like fruits with a distinct clove-like flavour. Fittingly, it is also known as the clove lilly pilly.

A hardy rainforest tree, the riberry's native distribution is the volcanic and sandy soils of subtropical northern New South Wales to northern Queensland. Like the common lilly pilly, the riberry is a popular and widely grown landscaping plant for domestic gardens, but it is also now being grown commercially as a bushfood.

Enjoyed by Indigenous Australians as a sweet and juicy treat, riberries were also valued for their immune-strengthening and cold-fighting properties as well as other nutritional benefits. The fruit was also said to have been crushed into a pulp and used to treat ear infections.

Just 100 g of riberries contains over 50% of the daily recommended intake of folate, otherwise known as B12, a vitamin necessary for healthy red blood cell production and particularly important for vegetarians, vegans and pregnant women. Riberries are also rich in antioxidants, manganese, magnesium, potassium, copper, calcium and vitamin E.

These small pear-shaped fruits have a spicy, clove-like flavour with a refreshingly tart citrus edge and can be used as you would a juniper berry. Unlike the common lilly pilly, riberries can be eaten whole without the need to remove the seeds. They can be eaten fresh from the tree and work particularly well in conserves, smoothies and salads. Riberries are available in frozen form year-round.

SPICED APPLE & RIBERRY CHIA PUDDING

SERVES 2

Tender spiced apples, plus plump riberries – with their clove-like flavour – are the stars in this satisfying dessert. Extra quantities of the creamy chia pudding are a great stand-by to have in the fridge for a quick breakfast.

Chia pudding

2 cups unsweetened coconut milk
½ teaspoon vanilla extract
2 tablespoons maple syrup
2 teaspoons maca powder
1 teaspoon Kakadu plum powder
1 teaspoon ground cinnamon
½ cup chia seeds

Spiced apple & riberry

4 granny smith apples, peeled, cored and diced
1 tablespoon lemon juice
2 tablespoons riberries, fresh or frozen
½ teaspoon ground cinnamon
¼ teaspoon freshly grated nutmeg
½ teaspoon vanilla extract
1 tablespoon maple syrup
¼ cup water
fresh fruit to serve (optional)

To make the chia pudding, combine the coconut milk, vanilla extract, maple syrup, maca powder, Kakadu plum powder and cinnamon in a blender and blend until combined. Pour the mixture into a large bowl and stir in the chia seeds. Cover and let soak in the fridge for at least 2 hours.

To make the stewed fruit, put the apples and lemon juice in a large saucepan, then add the riberries, spices, vanilla extract, maple syrup and water. Bring to a boil, then turn the heat down to a gentle simmer. Cover the saucepan and simmer for 10 minutes, stirring occasionally. Remove from the heat and let cool.

To serve, fill a jar or bowl with the spiced stewed fruit and chia pudding. Top with fresh fruit, if using.

ALTERNATIVELY

Coconut milk can be replaced with your choice of milk.

RIVER MINT

Mentha australis

This rambling, sweet-smelling herb, a relative to the common mint, can be found flourishing in the wild along riverbanks and edging swamps, rightly earning it the name river mint.

Sometimes known as native mint, river mint thrives in cool, damp environments, particularly in shaded areas, and is found across most of south-eastern Australia. This attractive and fragrant herb is now being commercially grown around the country for its various culinary uses.

Aboriginal people traditionally valued river mint for its refreshing, cooling flavour, but it also had wider applications. It was found to help relieve cold symptoms and stomach upsets when ingested in the form of a tea and the leaves were crushed and sniffed to help relieve headaches. To impart flavour, river mint was used to line earth ovens, a method of cooking food over coals and hot rocks in a sand-covered pit.

Like other varieties of mint, river mint contains rosmarinic acid, a natural compound with potent antioxidant, anti-inflammatory, antimicrobial and chemopreventive properties. It is also rich in menthol, a natural decongestant and reliever of indigestion. Due to its delightfully pungent aroma, river mint has also found use in cosmetic and aromatherapy products such as soaps and candles.

With a strong smell and punchy flavour somewhere between peppermint and spearmint, river mint adds a vibrant tone to both sweet and savoury dishes such as salads, sauces, cocktails and chocolates. Add a handful of leaves to boiling water and steep for 5–10 minutes for a relaxing, after-dinner tea. River mint is widely available in fresh or dried form year-round and may be frozen for up to 3 months.

RIVER MINT, BANANA, CACAO & MATCHA SMOOTHIE

SERVES 2

River mint has an amazing flavour and aroma of peppermint that really shines through in this quick and simple smoothie.

- 3 frozen bananas, chopped
- 3 fresh river mint leaves
- 1 handful baby spinach
- 4 tablespoons cacao nibs
- 2 teaspoons matcha powder
- 1 teaspoon vanilla extract
- 1 cup almond milk
- 2 teaspoons maca powder (optional)

ALTERNATIVELY

Use your milk preference instead of almond milk.

Put all the ingredients into a blender and pulse until smooth and combined. Serve immediately.

NOTE

River mint has a very strong flavour, so a little goes a long way. Try one river mint leaf if you prefer a less minty flavour.

ROSELLA

Hibiscus sabdariffa

An introduced species native to West Africa, the rosella or roselle has been adopted as one of Australia's most treasured plants and bushfood delicacies. The fast-growing open shrub grows to about 2 metres with large pale yellow to pink flowers and trademark bright red calyces – the outer layers that enclose and protect the flower – dotted along on the stem.

Now found on most continents and known by over 40 different names, rosella flowers, as they're commonly referred to in Australia, favour the dry rainforests and woodlands of eastern Queensland, New South Wales and the Northern Territory. They are now also commercially cultivated to great success and exported in various forms to over 50 countries.

The rosella was a particularly valuable plant to Indigenous Australians because of its strong but flexible fibre. The bast fibre was taken from the inner bark of the stem and was particularly useful in making nets and dilly bags, a traditional woven bag used in food gathering. Today rosella fibre is used, sometimes with jute, to make carpets, rope and paper. In addition to its practical uses to Indigenous Australians, the fleshy red calyces were eaten raw or cooked as a valuable source of dietary fibre and vitamin C.

The calyx of the rosella is a known source of anthocyanins, a flavonoid antioxidant responsible for its brilliant red hue. Anthocyanins have been linked with lowering blood pressure and cholesterol, boosting cognitive function and cancer prevention. Rosellas have also long been used in herbal medicine as a natural remedy for coughs and colds due to their vitamin C content and anti-inflammatory and antibacterial properties.

Rosellas have a tart, citric flavour somewhere between that of rhubarb and raspberry, with a sweet, subtle aroma. These beautiful flower heads can be made into a tasty jam or relish and work fantastically in drinks and dessert recipes. Due to the very short shelf life of fresh rosellas, they are available mostly frozen or dried and can be sourced in both forms year-round.

ROSELLA JAM BAKELESS LAMINGTONS

MAKES 10

This take on the iconic lamington utilises the tart, rhubarb flavour of rosella flowers in a jam that works just as well on toast or scones.

Base

1 cup almond meal
1 cup raw cashews (soaked for at least 30 minutes)
2 cups desiccated coconut
1 cup water
¼ cup rice malt syrup
2 tablespoons coconut oil

Rosella jam

2 cups rosella flowers
1 tablespoon lemon juice
½ cup rice malt syrup
1 teaspoon vanilla extract

Chocolate coating

½ cup coconut oil
½ cup cacao powder
¼ cup rice malt syrup
1 cup desiccated coconut, plus extra for coating

To make the lamington base, add the almond meal, soaked cashews, coconut, water, rice malt syrup and coconut oil to a blender and blend until combined.

Line a 12 × 27 cm baking tin with baking paper. Pour the base mixture evenly into the tin and freeze for a minimum of 3 hours.

To make the rosella jam, combine the rosella flowers, lemon juice, rice malt syrup and vanilla in a medium-sized saucepan and cook over a low-medium heat for 15 minutes. Stir frequently to avoid sticking. Let the mix cool a little, then blend until smooth. Cool jam completely.

To make the chocolate coating, add the coconut oil, cacao powder and rice malt syrup to a small saucepan. Cook over a medium heat for 3–5 minutes, stirring frequently until the mixture is totally combined and smooth. Pour the mix into a large bowl.

To construct the lamingtons, remove the chilled base carefully from the baking tin and cut it into 10 even rectangles. Prepare a large plate with desiccated coconut for rolling and place alongside the bowl of chocolate coating. Dunk each piece into the chocolate coating, then roll in the desiccated coconut. Repeat this for all the pieces.

Carefully cut each coated piece in half lengthwise. Use a butterknife to spread enough of the jam to generously cover one half and place the other on top. Gently press to bind both halves together. Repeat for all the pieces.

Put the lamingtons in an airtight container in the freezer to firm up for a few hours. Let them defrost for 30–60 minutes before serving.

SALTBUSH

Atriplex nummularia

If you've ever been lucky enough to have travelled across the Nullarbor, the squat blue-grey form of saltbush, or old man saltbush, will be no stranger to you. While commonly used as a fodder plant for livestock, recent years have seen saltbush become increasingly popular in the kitchens of some of the country's top chefs.

Highly adaptable and fast-growing, particularly after summer rain, this evergreen shrub can be found all over Australia's dry inland areas and is just one of over 60 different native species. A particularly palatable form, developed from several remnant species, is now commercially grown and readily available.

While the leaves of the saltbush themselves are fire retardant, the woody branches were commonly used by Aboriginal people as firewood. The seeds of the plant were also ground and roasted to make damper while the leaves were used as a wrap when cooking meat or fish. As a bush medicine, the salty leaves were applied topically as a treatment for cuts and other minor wounds.

Rich in minerals including calcium and magnesium, saltbush is also a great source of antioxidants, vitamin E and protein. Due to the plant's ability to store salt within its leaves, ground saltbush can be used as a healthy low-sodium table salt substitute.

The leaves of the saltbush, which are similar to English spinach but with a saltier flavour, can be eaten fresh or blanched and make a great salad base or dish on their own when stir-fried with garlic and tamari. The dried leaves can also be ground and blended with other spices to create a delicious seasoning. Saltbush leaves are available year-round fresh, dried or as part of a seasoning mix.

SALTBUSH DUKKAH CAULIFLOWER STEAKS

SERVES 2

This recipe makes more than enough dukkah, for good reason. Serve leftover dukkah as an accompaniment to roast vegetables, with bread and olive oil, on hummus or sprinkled on salads.

Dukkah
⅓ cup macadamia nuts
⅓ cup pistachio nuts
⅓ cup hazelnuts
⅓ cup sesame seeds
3 tablespoons cumin seeds
2 tablespoons coriander seeds
2 teaspoons dried saltbush
1 teaspoon dried lemon myrtle
1 teaspoon ground mountain pepper leaf
½ teaspoon salt

3 garlic cloves, crushed
3 tablespoons olive oil
1 large cauliflower
pomegranate seeds, to garnish
thinly sliced Lebanese (short) cucumber, to garnish

Hummus
2 × 400 g tinned chickpeas
½ cup tahini
1-2 garlic cloves
juice of 1 lemon
½ teaspoon ground cumin
salt and pepper to taste

To make the dukkah, toast the macadamia nuts, pistachio nuts and hazelnuts in a dry frying pan over low heat. Cook until golden and aromatic, then remove from the heat and let cool for a few minutes. Blitz the toasted nuts briefly in a blender, creating a coarse mixture.

Add the sesame seeds to the same dry frying pan and cook on low heat until golden. Shake the pan frequently and take care not to burn them. Set aside. Repeat with the cumin and coriander seeds, toasting until aromatic. Combine the toasted cumin and coriander seeds and blend in a blender until powdered.

In a large bowl combine the toasted nuts, sesame seeds, ground cumin and coriander with the saltbush, lemon myrtle, pepper leaf and salt. Mix until well combined. Set aside until needed.

Preheat the oven to 200°C (400°F). Line a large baking tray with baking paper.

Combine the garlic and olive oil in a large mixing bowl. Trim and cut the cauliflower into 3 cm pieces, then transfer them to the bowl with the garlic and oil. Sprinkle over 3 tablespoons of the dukkah and toss the pieces gently so that all sides of the cauliflower are well coated. Transfer the cauliflower to the baking tray and roast for 35-40 minutes, turning once. Leave to cool slightly.

To make the hummus, drain the chickpeas and combine with the other ingredients in a blender. Blend until smooth and season with salt and pepper, adding a touch of water if needed to thin the consistency.

Spread a generous quantity of hummus on a plate and top with the cauliflower pieces. Garnish with pomegranate seeds and thinly shaved slices of cucumber, if using. Serve immediately.

NOTE
Keep dukkah in an airtight container for up to a month.

SAMPHIRE

Salicornia europaea

Allegedly a culinary favourite of Henry VIII and mentioned in Shakespeare's *King Lear*, this salty, crunchy seashore vegetable was something of a celebrity long before it made its presence known on the Australian fine dining scene.

Six genera of samphire naturally occur in Australia, forming dense, low mats along the coastlines and salt marshes of the southern states. It grows as thin, upright stems with fleshy sections, very like a seaweed. Also known as glasswort or the asparagus of the sea, it is the European species of samphire, *S. europaea*, that is commercially grown in saltwater channel plots and seaweed composts in South Australia and Victoria and is now sold to retail outlets both at home and abroad.

Samphire was a prized bushfood due to its nutritional value and abundance. Aboriginal people valued the tender shoots of samphire for their salty tang but also as a portable source of liquid that could be taken inland. Another species of samphire, blackseed samphire, was utilised for its seeds, which were ground and made into a damper.

As well as being high in vitamins A, B2 and C, samphire contains fucoidan, a substance found in sea vegetables, seaweeds and algae, that is used medicinally to treat high blood pressure. Samphire is also a valuable source of iron, calcium, potassium and phytochemicals, said to protect the liver and heart and aid in DNA repair.

With its delicious and naturally salty flavour and crisp texture, samphire is best used as one might use green vegetables like asparagus or green beans: blanched, sautéed quickly with garlic and onion, added to stir-fries and salads or pickled. Samphire is available fresh most of the year.

PICKLED SAMPHIRE & MIXED VEGETABLES

MAKES 1 JAR

Samphire is perfect for pickling, with its asparagus-like texture and taste. Be sure to let the pickles settle for at least a week to really allow the flavours to develop. Great served in sandwiches, macro bowls or straight from the jar.

2 cups samphire
2 carrots, peeled and julienned
½ red capsicum julienned
1 Lebanese (short) cucumber, julienned
1 jalapeno chilli, halved lengthways
4 garlic cloves, peeled and halved
2 sprigs dill
1 tablespoon coriander seeds
1 teaspoon mountain pepper berries
1 teaspoon yellow mustard seeds
1 litre glass jar, sterilised

Pickling liquid
2½ cups water
1 tablespoon salt
½ cup apple cider vinegar
5 tablespoons rice malt syrup

While you're preparing the vegetables, bring a large saucepan of water to the boil. Drop the samphire into the boiling water and blanch for 1–2 minutes. Strain in a colander, then add the samphire to a large bowl of cold water to stop it from cooking further. Drain and set aside.

To make the pickling liquid, combine all the ingredients in a large non-reactive saucepan and bring to the boil. Reduce the heat and simmer for 5 minutes.

Transfer the carrots, capsicum, cucumber and jalapenos to the glass jar, arranging the pieces vertically and filling any gaps with samphire. Tuck in the garlic, dill and spices.

Carefully pour over the warm pickling liquid and let cool. Seal the jar firmly and refrigerate when cold. This pickle will keep for up to 3 weeks.

SANDALWOOD NUT

Santalum spicatum

A close second to the macadamia nut as Australia's favourite nut, the hard-shelled sandalwood nut and the small yet robust tree from which it is borne, are highly valued the world over for their use in skin care products, aromatherapy, medicine and furniture making.

The sandalwood tree is hemiparasitic, meaning it gains some of its nourishment from a host plant, in this case often the roots of *Acacia* trees. One of four highly sought-after *Santalum* species found in Australia, this particular variety is native to central and southern Western Australia, extending into South Australia. It is the most planted commercial tree crop in Western Australia with more than 30,000 hectares of plantations and is one of the state's most important exports.

Utilised by Indigenous Australians for its medicinal and cosmetic properties, the oil from sandalwood nuts was extracted and commonly used to moisturise the skin and hair. Sandalwood oil is known for its significant antimicrobial and anti-inflammatory properties and was traditionally made into a healing balm that was applied to sores and boils. The bark of the tree was also made use of and infused to make a drinkable remedy for cold symptoms.

Sandalwood nuts are low in saturated fats and rich in omega-9 fatty acids, protein and dietary fibre. They are also said to be able to help balance blood sugar levels and help prevent type 2 diabetes. Sandalwood nut oil contains high levels of ximenynic acid, a fatty acid with anti-inflammatory properties that has become a popular ingredient in skin care products for its ability to improve skin elasticity. It is now readily available as an essential oil.

Sandalwood nuts are encased in a hard shell that requires a nut cracker to open. The perfectly round nuts within are delicious raw or roasted, with a subtle flavour reminiscent of hazelnut. They make a great addition to muesli, dukkah or homemade crackers and are available shelled – raw, roasted or flavoured – all year round.

SANDALWOOD NUT & SEED CRACKERS

MAKES 20–24

These moreish crackers are great as a snack or topped with cashew cheese, avocado and tomato for something a little more substantial.

- 2 tablespoons ground chia seeds
- 6 tablespoons water
- ½ cup uncooked quinoa
- ¼ cup raw sandalwood nuts, shelled
- ¼ cup macadamia nuts
- ¼ cup pepitas
- ¼ cup sesame seeds
- ½ teaspoon salt
- ½ teaspoon onion powder
- ½ teaspoon garlic powder
- ½ teaspoon dried mountain pepper leaf
- ½ teaspoon dried native basil
- ½ teaspoon nutritional yeast

Preheat the oven to 175°C (340°F).

Combine the ground chia with the water, stir and let sit for 15 minutes.

Cook the quinoa as per the packet instructions, then set aside and let cool.

Add the sandalwood nuts, macadamia nuts and pepitas to a blender and pulse until roughly chopped.

Combine the chopped nuts and pepitas, sesame seeds, quinoa, chia mixture and all remaining ingredients in a large bowl and mix well.

Line two baking trays with baking paper and divide the mixture between them. Using an additional sheet of baking paper, press down and evenly flatten out the mixture on each tray until it is 3–5 mm thick.

With a sharp knife, lightly score the cracker mix into 10 or 12 pieces per tray.

Bake in the oven for 50–60 minutes until crackers are golden, swapping and turning trays at the halfway mark. Leave the crackers on the trays to cool completely before separating. Store them in an airtight container for up to 5 days.

Serve with our Lemon Myrtle & Dill Cashew Cheese (page 93)

NOTE

We recommend buying the sandalwood nuts already shelled. If you prefer them whole, you'll need to use a nut cracker to remove the shell.

SEA PARSLEY

Apium prostratum

Described by renowned Australian chef Simon Bryant as being 'a bit like parsley on steroids', this perennial coastal herb with soft, dark green leaves is also commonly known as sea celery.

Endemic to the rugged terrain of much of Australia's southern coastline, this hardy, low-growing herb can be found on dunes, cliff faces and growing right down to the seashore where it is often submerged by high tides. Sea parsley has become a popular ingredient with home cooks as a handy and easy-to-establish pot plant and is now commercially cultivated as well.

Sea parsley was favoured by Indigenous Australians for its immune-boosting qualities – now attributed to its high vitamin C content – and was commonly made into an elixir. Its herbaceous aroma added a welcome flavour boost to cooked meals and was also reportedly used to waterproof canoes.

This close relative of European parsley shares much of its associated nutritional qualities, including being rich in vitamins C and K and offering a good source of vitamin A, folate and iron. Sea parsley also contains chlorophyll, a natural detoxifier for liver and kidney health, which has in recent times seen it used in health and skin care products.

Sea parsley has a distinctive salty, parsley-celery flavour and may be used in place of regular parsley or celery tops. It is best utilised in savoury dishes such as soups, pasta sauces, salad dressings and stews; if collected, the seeds can be used as a spice similar to fennel seeds. Sea parsley is available fresh from bushfood retailers all year round.

SWEET POTATO FALAFEL WITH SEA PARSLEY TABBOULEH

MAKES 20

These healthy, oven-baked falafel are well worth the effort and work fantastically wrapped up in flatbread with the sea parsley tabbouleh and hummus. We like to make a double batch and freeze some for later.

Falafel

1 large sweet potato
½ red onion, chopped
3 garlic cloves, crushed
1 green chilli, finely chopped
handful coriander, leaves and stems
handful sea parsley
400 g tinned chickpeas
1 teaspoon ground cumin
½ teaspoon ground mountain pepper leaf
½ cup besan flour
juice of ½ lemon
¼ cup sesame seeds, for sprinkling
salt and pepper, to taste

Tabbouleh

1 cup quinoa
2 cups water
1 stock cube
2 handfuls sea parsley, finely chopped
1 handful mint, finely chopped
12 cherry tomatoes, finely chopped
juice of 1 lemon
1 tablespoon olive oil

lemon wedges, to serve
hummus, to serve
sliced avocado, to serve (optional)

Preheat the oven to 180°C (350°F). Line two baking trays with baking paper.

Wrap the sweet potato in aluminium foil and bake for 1 hour or until it feels soft. Remove from the oven, unwrap and leave to cool, then scoop out and roughly chop the flesh, discarding the skin.

To make the falafel, combine the sweet potato flesh and all the other ingredients, except for the sesame seeds, in a blender and blitz until combined – this may need to be done in batches.

Transfer the falafel mixture to a bowl and season well with salt and freshly ground black pepper. Using wet hands, roll the mixture into rounds the size of golf balls and sprinkle with sesame seeds. Place the falafel onto the baking trays and bake for 35 minutes, swapping and turning trays at the halfway mark.

To make the tabbouleh, first rinse and drain the quinoa. Add it to a saucepan with the water and stock cube and bring to the boil, then cover and reduce to a low simmer for 15 minutes or until all of the liquid is absorbed. Leave to cool.

Combine the cooked quinoa with the sea parsley, mint, tomatoes, lemon juice and olive oil in a large bowl. Stir until everything is well combined.

Serve the falafel warm or cold, with some tabbouleh on the side, a dollop of hummus and a lemon wedge.

SEABLITE

Suaeda australis

This coastal succulent is just one of around 110 species of *Suaeda*, or seablite, which can be found around the world growing along coastlines and estuaries. Used in cooking for centuries and valued for its easy harvesting, crisp texture and natural salty flavour, the sodium-rich ashes of several species of seablite native to Europe were also used in medieval times as an ingredient in glass-making; today it is commonly called glasswort.

Native seablite, which is sometimes referred to as sea spray in Australia for the environments in which it thrives, is native to the shorelines and salt marshes of most Australian states. It is a low-growing groundcover, with short, pale green, fleshy leaves, well adapted to its conditions. Due to its rise in popularity as a bushfood ingredient in cooking, seablite is now sustainably grown by several commercial operators.

Seablite was a valuable and readily available source of essential vitamins to Indigenous Australians. The succulent stems were commonly eaten raw or cooked as an accompaniment to other meals. Seablite is now known to contain concentrations of vitamins A and E and may have antiviral and antibacterial potential. It is also a source of polyphenols, naturally occurring compounds found in plants that contain high antioxidant and cancer-preventing properties.

The naturally salty, tender stems of seablite have long been used throughout Europe in the same manner as green beans and may be eaten raw, steamed, stir-fried or blanched for 1–2 minutes. It is available fresh year-round from a variety of growers.

SEABLITE RICE PAPER ROLLS

MAKES 10

Rice paper rolls are a great way of using up whatever vegetables you have in the fridge. The raw seablite adds a pop of natural saltiness and crunch to this recipe, ideal for the warmer months.

Spicy tahini sauce
3 tablespoons tahini
4 tablespoons tamari or soy sauce
1 garlic clove, crushed
juice of ½ lime
1 teaspoon rice wine vinegar
1 teaspoon sriracha
1 teaspoon sesame oil
2 tablespoons water

Rice paper rolls
500 g firm tofu
2-3 tablespoons coconut oil
1 cup seablite, picked into small sprigs
2 large carrots
1 Lebanese (short) cucumber
1 red capsicum
¼ red cabbage
2 avocados
4 spring onions, finely chopped
1 handful chopped coriander leaves
1 packet 22 cm rice paper wrappers

To make the tahini sauce, combine all the ingredients in a small bowl and mix until incorporated. Set aside until needed.

To make the rice paper rolls, start by cutting the tofu into 1 cm thick slices, then pat dry with some paper towel.

Heat the coconut oil in a large frying pan over medium heat. Add the tofu slices and fry until golden. Remove from the heat and drain on more paper towel. Cut the tofu into 1 cm width strips.

Slice the carrots, cucumber and capsicum into thin sticks, keeping everything similar lengths. Shred the red cabbage finely. Slice the avocado lengthwise into thin strips.

Assemble all the prepared vegetables, herbs and tofu together on a tray on the workbench. You need to work systematically once assembly is under way.

Fill a large bowl with warm water. Carefully dip and rotate a sheet of rice paper into the bowl of water, submerging for about 15 seconds. Remove from the water, drain off the excess and put on a large dinner plate or damp tea towel.

Arrange the seablite, carrot, cucumber, capsicum, cabbage, avocado, spring onions, coriander and tofu along the middle of the rice paper round, making sure not to overfill it. Leave a foldable edge at each side. Fold in the sides and roll firmly. Repeat with the other wrappers.

Rice paper rolls are best eaten fresh. Serve with the spicy tahini sauce.

STRAWBERRY GUM

Eucalyptus olida

Another member of the Australian native eucalypt family, strawberry gum is renowned for its red-tinted leaves and incredible berry aroma, which has earned it the nickname the 'forestberry herb'. The complex aroma from its essential oil - cherries, menthol, cinnamon – has made it a valuable essential oil and ingredient in perfumery.

Tolerant to frost conditions down to -8°C, strawberry gum has a very restricted natural range, being local to the woodlands of the Northern Tablelands in New South Wales where it can grow up to 20 metres tall. Considered a threatened species in the wild, strawberry gum is now grown commercially for its essential oil and unique spice qualities.

Strawberry gum leaves were prized by Aboriginal people for their sweet, berry flavour when chewed. The leaves were also used as a bush medicine; laid wet over a fire, an aromatic smoke would be released and inhaled to help soothe upset stomachs.

A rich source of antioxidants, strawberry gum leaves also contain antibiotic and antifungal properties that assist in balancing the microflora or bacteria of the stomach, promoting good gut health. Perhaps best known for its use in respiratory health, the active ingredients found in all species of eucalyptus leaves act as expectorants, which help treat and prevent respiratory ailments, clear sinuses and generally aid breathing.

In cooking, aromatic strawberry gum leaves are an incredible flavour enhancer due to their high concentration of methyl cinnamate. They are a particularly good addition to recipes containing cooked fruit such as jams, crumbles and pies. You can also steep leaves for 10 minutes in boiling water to make an all-round tea tonic. Strawberry gum leaves are available dried – whole, flakes or ground – from a variety of bushfood stockists. It's also sold as an essential oil.

STRAWBERRY GUM JAM DROPS

MAKES 20-25

The addition of even a single strawberry gum leaf will intensify the flavour of berry-based jams and desserts. The lilly pilly adds a citrus note that also complements the strawberries. Use up any leftover jam on toast or scones.

Strawberry gum jam

- 250 g strawberries, fresh or frozen, diced
- ½ cup lilly pillies, fresh or frozen, diced
- 1 teaspoon vanilla extract
- ¼ cup rice malt syrup
- 1 strawberry gum leaf, whole
- 2 tablespoons chia seeds

Biscuits

- 2 cups almond flour
- ½ teaspoon gluten-free baking powder
- ½ teaspoon ground wattleseed
- ⅓ cup rice malt syrup
- 1 teaspoon vanilla extract

ALTERNATIVELY

If you don't have rice malt syrup, use the same quantity of maple syrup as a substitute.

To make the jam, add the strawberries, lilly pillies, vanilla, rice malt syrup and strawberry gum leaf to a heavy-based medium saucepan. Cook on a low heat for 20 minutes, stirring frequently, until thickened. Remove from the heat and let cool a little before removing the strawberry gum leaf and stirring in the chia seeds.

To make the biscuits, preheat the oven to 175°C (340°F) and line two baking trays with baking paper.

Add the almond flour, baking powder, ground wattleseed, rice malt syrup and vanilla to a large bowl and mix to combine. Mix well until the mixture forms a dough.

Pulling small pieces from the dough, roll into 3 cm balls using your hands and put them on the baking trays. Be sure to leave at least 1cm between each round of dough.

Using your index finger, make a slight indent in the middle of each biscuit, then spoon a small dollop of jam into them.

Bake for 15 minutes or until slightly golden. Remove from the oven and leave to cool completely on a wire rack.

NOTE

This will make more than enough jam for the biscuits. Store the remainder in a sterilised jar in the fridge.

NATIVE TAMARIND

Diploglottis australis

This tall native rainforest tree is known for its open canopy and large, palm-like foliage but is perhaps better known for the vibrant orange fruits found growing high up on its trunk – a magnet for a variety of bird species.

Native tamarind occurs naturally in the subtropics of Australia's east coast, from south-east Queensland to northern New South Wales. It grows up to 35 metres tall in the wild and is widely used as a rainforest revegetation tree as well as a specimen tree. Native tamarind is commercially cultivated for its ornamental qualities and its juicy, tangy fruit.

These striking, orange-yellow fruits have long been enjoyed as a refreshing bushfood by Indigenous Australians and were generally eaten freshly fallen from the tree. The fruit was also used to make a sweet drink by removing the flesh from the seed, pulping it and mixing it with water.

Packed with immune-boosting vitamin C and essential minerals, the fruit of the native tamarind also contains flavonoids, naturally occurring antioxidants with anti-inflammatory properties that aid in protecting the body from the harmful effects of free radicals. Native tamarind is also a valuable source of amino acids, able to assist in improving muscle growth and reversing muscle breakdown.

Despite its name, native tamarind is not related to the common tamarind and is in fact related to the lychee. Native tamarind fruit has a sweet yet slightly sour flavour and has been likened to green mangoes in taste. It can be used in both sweet and savoury dishes such as jams, chutneys, marinades, sauces and cocktails. The fruit is available in frozen form as well as a paste.

NATIVE TAMARIND COCONUT CURRY NOODLE SOUP

SERVES 4-6

Native tamarind is milder than common tamarind varieties, which can be rather sour. Here, native tamarind adds a distinctive tang and citrus flavour to the curry paste that forms the base for this laksa-like soup, packed with vegetables and goodness.

Curry paste

1 red onion, roughly chopped
4 tablespoons lemongrass, white part only, finely chopped
3 tablespoons freshly grated ginger
2 tablespoons native tamarind paste
6 cloves garlic
2 teaspoons ground turmeric
1 green chilli, chopped
½ cup coriander leaves and stems
1 teaspoon coriander seeds
1 teaspoon cumin seeds
1 teaspoon ground cinnamon
1 teaspoon sweet paprika
1 tablespoon tamari or soy sauce
3 tablespoons lime juice

Soup

200 g packet thin rice noodles
1 tablespoon coconut oil
3 cups coconut milk
4 cups vegetable stock
1 tablespoon sesame oil
1 cup carrots, finely sliced
1 cup mushrooms, finely sliced
1 cup broccoli, chopped into small florets
2 cups green beans, chopped
1 cup snow peas, trimmed
1 handful fresh coriander leaves, to garnish
lime wedges, to serve (optional)

To make the curry paste, combine all the ingredients in a blender and blend until smooth. Set aside.

Bring a large saucepan of water to the boil and add the rice noodles. Stir well to keep noodles separated. Cook for 2 minutes, drain and set aside.

Heat the coconut oil in a large saucepan and add the curry paste. Cook over medium heat for 2 minutes, until aromatic, then add the coconut milk, vegetable stock and sesame oil. Bring to the boil, then reduce the heat and simmer for 5 minutes. Add the carrots, mushrooms, broccoli and beans and cook for a further 10 minutes. Add the snow peas to the soup and cook for 5 minutes. Adjust the seasoning to taste.

To serve, divide the noodles amongst the bowls and top with the hot soup. Serve immediately, garnished with fresh coriander and lime wedges, if using.

NOTE

You may like to balance the native tamarind paste with a couple of tablespoons of coconut sugar in the soup.

Keep the noodles separate from the soup until ready to serve as they will soak up the liquid.

NATIVE THYME

Prostranthera rotundifolia

Covered in beautiful lilac-coloured flowers, this attractive small shrub is confusingly named native thyme but commonly called roundleaf mint. With its potent minty aroma and place in the *Prostanthera* or mint bush genus, the latter name would seem to be a more apt one but its tiny, spaced green leaves do indeed bear a resemblance to thyme.

This strongly aromatic bush herb is widespread in Australia but particularly favours the cool climates of south-east New South Wales, eastern Victoria and Tasmania, where it can be found growing along riverbanks. Native thyme has become a popular garden plant for its hardiness and adaptability, particularly in hedging, reaching up to 2 metres. It is also grown in commercial shadehouses for its essential oil and culinary uses.

Native thyme was appreciated more for its medicinal properties than its flavour by Indigenous Australians. They traditionally made use of the antibiotic properties of the plant by infusing the leaves and twigs in hot water to make a tonic that was used to soothe headaches and colds, as well as dysentery and fever.

The volatile oil extracted from the leaves of native thyme is rich in thymol, a naturally occurring compound with proven antibacterial and antifungal properties that amongst many other uses has been shown to relieve gastrointestinal pain, soothe throat infections and treat various ailments of the skin. Native thyme oil is now an ingredient in various topical ointments and antibacterial mouthwashes.

The small, round leaves of native thyme add a delicious herbaceous element to dishes, with an intense flavour of thyme and mint, similar to an Italian seasoning blend. Native thyme works well in tomato-based sauces, soups, salad dressings and as a seasoning on roasted vegetables. It's available dried or fresh year-round from a variety of bushfood stockists.

BREAKFAST SCRAMBLE WITH NATIVE THYME

SERVES 4

The native thyme adds a fragrant herbal dimension to this hearty breakfast scramble. The black salt – usually from India – is definitely worth adding if you're able to source it. Its slightly sulphurous aroma is decidedly egg-like and delicious.

Cashew cream

1 cup raw cashews (soaked for at least 30 minutes)

1 tablespoon apple cider vinegar

1 cup water

pinch of salt

Spice mix

4 tablespoons nutritional yeast

1 teaspoon sweet paprika

3 sprigs fresh native thyme, or 1 teaspoon dried

1 teaspoon dried mountain pepper leaf

1 teaspoon turmeric

1 teaspoon black salt or ½ teaspoon salt

½ cup unsweetened almond milk

Scramble

1 tablespoon coconut oil

1 onion, diced

1 red chilli, deseeded

2 garlic cloves, crushed

500 g firm tofu

2 spring onions, chopped, to garnish

avocado, thinly sliced, to serve

cherry tomatoes, halved, to serve

toast, to serve

ALTERNATIVELY

You can use ¼ teaspoon of freshly ground black pepper instead of the mountain pepper leaf.

Begin by making the cashew cream. Combine all the ingredients in a blender and blitz until smooth, then set aside.

To make the spice mix, combine the nutritional yeast, paprika, native thyme, pepper leaf, turmeric and salt with the almond milk and whisk until combined. Set aside for a few minutes.

To make the scramble, heat the coconut oil in a medium-sized frying pan and add the onion, cooking for 5 minutes until translucent. Add the chilli and garlic and cook for a further minute.

Crumble the tofu in small pieces into the pan, stirring until well combined. Let the tofu brown a little around the edges.

Add the spice mix to the scramble, mixing well until the tofu is fully coated. Cook for 3 minutes.

Pour in the cashew cream and stir well, cooking for a further 8–10 minutes or until most of the liquid has been absorbed. Add the chopped spring onion in the last 5 minutes, leaving aside a little for garnish.

Check the seasoning and serve immediately, topped with spring onions. We like to serve this with sliced avocado, cherry tomatoes and toast for a full breakfast.

WARRIGAL GREENS

Tetragonia tetragoniodes

Warrigal greens, a name seemingly made up from two earlier names given to this creeping groundcover – warrigal cabbage and Botany Bay greens – was the first Australian native food plant to be introduced into Europe, when botanist Joseph Banks took seeds to England in the 1770s.

Native not just to Australia but also to New Zealand, Argentina, Chile and Japan, this hardy spinach-like plant grows in the sandy beach and salt marsh environments of the east coast of Australia. This highly prized leafy green is now sustainably grown by several nurseries around the country and supplied to restaurants and bushfood distributors.

Though there is not much reported use of warrigal greens as bush tucker by Aboriginal Australians, this not-quite cousin of English spinach was found by early explorers to be an effective scurvy preventative due to the high levels of vitamin C contained in the leaves.

Loaded with antioxidants and anti-inflammatory properties, warrigal greens are also a great plant-based source of iron, making them particularly valuable to vegetarians and vegans. The small, diamond-shaped leaves are also a known source of vitamins A, B, C, E and K as well as minerals potassium, phosphorus and calcium.

Given its similarity to English spinach, warrigal greens make a fantastic filling in pies, as a base for salads and made into pesto. It is important to note, though, that the leaves of warrigal greens do contain toxic oxalates, so while it is fine to eat the young leaves raw, older leaves should be blanched for 1-2 minutes or boiled before adding to recipes. Warrigal greens may be sourced fresh year-round.

WARRIGAL GREENS & KALE PIE

SERVES 4-6

This recipe is our take on Lily's dad Toly's famous spinach pie. Here, warrigal greens are used in place of English spinach, with some kale thrown in for extra goodness.

- 1.5 kg mixed warrigal greens and kale leaves, stems discarded, roughly chopped
- 3 teaspoons egg replacer
- 6 tablespoons water
- 1 tablespoon coconut oil
- 2 onions, diced
- 5 garlic cloves, crushed
- 2 teaspoons freshly grated nutmeg
- 3 teaspoons vegetable stock
- 200 g almond feta
- 1 pack filo pastry
- 1 tablespoon sesame seeds

ALTERNATIVELY

3 eggs can be used instead of egg replacer

200 g of feta can be used instead of almond feta

Preheat the oven to 200°C (400°F).

Bring a large saucepan of water to the boil. Add the warrigal greens and kale to the water and blanch for 1 minute or until wilted. Remove the greens and drain well.

Add egg replacer and water to a bowl and whisk until combined. Set aside.

Heat the coconut oil in a large saucepan over low heat. Add the onions, then sauté gently for 5 minutes until translucent. Add the garlic and continue cooking for 1 minute. Add the warrigal greens, kale, nutmeg, vegetable stock and prepared egg replacer to the onion mixture and cook for another 5 minutes, mixing well. Remove from the heat and let cool.

Cut the almond feta into small cubes and gently stir through the pie filling.

To assemble the pie, grease and line a 23 × 33 cm pie dish with 3 sheets of filo pastry, then brush with olive oil. Repeat this process with another 3 sheets of pastry.

Spoon the pie filling onto the pastry and spread evenly. Layer 3 sheets of filo on top of the filling and brush with olive oil. Repeat with another 3 sheets. Sprinkle with sesame seeds.

Bake the pie for 40 minutes or until the pastry is golden. Rest for 10 minutes before slicing and serving.

Serve with our Davidson Plum Chilli Sauce (page 48).

NOTE

Almond feta is a delicious non-dairy alternative to feta, often marinated in olive oil and herbs. You can find it in health food stores.

Egg replacer is an eggless product used for binding and baking and is available in most supermarkets.

WATTLESEED

Acacia victoriae

The *Acacia* genus, or wattle, is made up of over 500 species found in most climate zones of Australia. While the gold blooms of one species, *A. pycnantha*, became Australia's floral emblem in 1988, Indigenous Australians have been eating the seeds of some 50 varieties of wattle for over 40,000 years.

One such species is *A. victoriae*, a widespread shrub-like tree native to subtropical and semi-arid regions of Western Australia, Central Australia, South Australia, New South Wales and Queensland. This is the variety most widely used in the bushfood industry, considered to have the most palatable and versatile seed. While wattleseed is still largely wild-harvested, commercial plantations produce an estimated four tonnes of wattleseed per year.

Traditionally, Aboriginal people had multiple uses for different parts of this versatile tree. They would collect and dry the seed pods, then extract the wattleseeds. The dried seeds were most commonly ground into flour and used to make a high-fibre damper. The bark of the wattle was brewed into a tea and drunk to soothe indigestion and inflammation. The high-tannin bark was also used to tan animal skins and poison fish. Wood from the wattle was also used to make items such as boomerangs, spears, digging sticks and clap sticks.

Wattleseeds are a low glycemic carbohydrate, meaning that they slowly release their sugars and can help to maintain steady blood sugar levels. They are also a very rich source of fibre, protein, calcium, potassium, iron, zinc, selenium and essential fatty acids.

When roasted, wattleseed has a delicious aroma and flavour of hazelnut and coffee. It can be used in the same way as coffee beans, serving as a good caffeine-free substitute. Try using it as an addition to baking and desserts such as breads, pancakes, brownies and tiramisu. Wattleseed has a remarkably long shelf life – up to 10 years – and is available roasted whole and ground and as an extract.

WATTLESEED TIRAMISU

SERVES 3-4

Wattleseed has an enticing aroma and flavour of roasted coffee, with a note of hazelnuts. Here it's used in the base and filling of this easy-to-make, caffeine-free alternative to regular tiramisu.

Base

1 cup raw macadamia nuts
½ cup dates, pitted
4 teaspoons ground wattleseed
pinch of salt

Topping

2 cups raw cashews (soaked for at least 30 minutes)
½ cup almond milk
¼ cup maple syrup
2 teaspoons ground wattleseed
1 teaspoon vanilla extract
1–2 tablespoons cacao powder, for dusting

To make the base, add macadamia nuts, dates, ground wattleseed and salt to a blender and blend until the mixture creates a crumbly paste. Set aside.

To make the topping, combine the cashews, almond milk, maple syrup, ground wattleseed and vanilla extract in a blender and blitz until smooth. Put to one side.

Spoon the base mixture into the bottom of small dessert bowls or mini mason jars so it is evenly spread. Press down firmly. Spoon on the topping and dust with cacao powder. Keep in the fridge for an hour before serving.

ALTERNATIVELY

Use your milk preference instead of almond milk.

GLOSSARY

ALMOND FLOUR AND ALMOND MEAL

Almond flour is made from ground blanched (skinless) almonds and is usually a fairly fine texture. Almond meal is a slightly coarser grind and can be blanched or unblanched. Both are nutritious gluten-free alternatives to wheat flour. Almond flour and meal is high in protein and is a valuable source of iron, magnesium, potassium and calcium. It is commonly used in gluten-free baking of cakes, biscuits and breads.

BESAN

Besan, also known as chickpea flour or gram flour, is made from finely ground chickpeas and is high in protein, potassium, zinc, iron, calcium and magnesium. It is a great gluten-free alternative for batters, flatbreads and fritters.

BLACK SALT

Also known as kala namak, black salt is a volcanic rock salt that has a strong smell and flavour of sulphur. It's commonly used in vegan dishes when trying to replicate the flavour and aroma of egg and is a valuable addition to curries, soups and vegan 'egg' recipes. Regular salt can be used in its place.

CHAGA MUSHROOMS

Found growing on birch trees throughout the northern hemisphere, chaga mushrooms are high in antioxidants and can help to reduce inflammation, support the immune system and combat some viruses. Chaga is also used to help reduce stress, increase energy and nourish the skin.

Chaga mushrooms are typically bought as a dried powder and used as a nutritional supplement. Chaga powder has a subtle flavour and is a beneficial addition to smoothies, warm drinks and baking.

CHIA SEEDS

Native to Mexico and Guatemala, chia seeds are a rich, plant-based source of omega-3 fatty acids, protein and antioxidants, making them particularly valuable to vegetarians and vegans. Chia seeds are a fantastic egg replacer, and work well in salads and smoothies.

COCONUT SUGAR

Coconut sugar, also called coconut palm sugar, is made from the sap of the coconut plant and has a flavour reminiscent of brown sugar, with a hint of coconut. It can be used wherever regular sugar is called for.

EGG REPLACER

Egg replacer is a commercially available powdered alternative to eggs, especially used for baking cakes, biscuits and breads. It is commonly made of potato or tapioca starch. It is available from most supermarkets.

FLAXSEEDS

Flaxseeds, or linseeds, are high in omega-3 fatty acids, fibre, B vitamins and magnesium. Flaxseeds are best consumed in ground form to fully utilise their health benefits, as this is easier for the body to digest.

Like chia seeds, flaxseeds form a gel-like consistency when added to water, which acts as a binder and a good replacement for eggs in baking. Flaxseeds can also be added to smoothies, muesli and salads.

MACA

Maca is a root vegetable native to Peru and is also known as Peruvian ginseng. Maca contains vitamins B, C and E, calcium, zinc, amino acids, iron, potassium and magnesium. It is said to help balance moods, increase energy, promote clear skin and reduce stress.

Usually available in ground form, maca powder has a malt-like flavour and is great in smoothies, raw desserts, muesli and drinks. You can cook it or add it to hot foods, but doing so will lessen its nutrient potency: best to consume it uncooked.

MATCHA

Matcha is finely ground (powdered) green tea and has been grown in Japan for 900 years. It is said to increase concentration and metabolism. Matcha boasts incredible antioxidant content as well as being a known source of vitamins A, B, C, E and K.

Traditionally, matcha is prepared with hot water to make a grassy-flavoured tea but it now also has a variety of culinary uses. Matcha can be added to desserts, smoothies, pancakes and savoury dishes.

NUTRITIONAL YEAST

This is an inactive yeast that has a nutty, cheesy flavour. It is a rich source of vitamin B12, which on a vegan diet is the only nutrient that is not easily obtained.

Nutritional yeast is bought in powder form and is commonly used as a cheese substitute. It can be used in much the same way as parmesan cheese: in vegan cheeses, sauces, dressings, baking and soups.

QUINOA

Quinoa is a seed, but can be prepared in much the same way as a grain. It is a valuable gluten-free alternative to rice and starchy grains and is packed with protein, fibre, iron, potassium, calcium, vitamin E and all of the essential amino acids. Quinoa can be used in salads and baking.

RAW CACAO

Raw cacao is super-rich in beneficial antioxidants because it has not been heat processed, unlike cocoa. Raw cacao also contains magnesium and vitamin C and is available as powder, paste and nibs. Use in chocolates, smoothies and desserts.

RAW CASHEWS

Raw cashews have a more subtle flavour than roasted cashews, and are rich in iron, copper, zinc and manganese. Soaking raw cashews and then blending them achieves a creamy consistency that is a great dairy-free alternative. They can be used in yoghurt, dressings, soups, sweet bases, and smoothies.

REISHI MUSHROOMS
These mushrooms have long been used in traditional Chinese medicine for their multitude of health benefits. Said to prolong life, reishi mushrooms can help in the treatment of high blood pressure, liver disorders, asthma and viral infections. They are also thought to help reduce stress and improve sleep.

Reishi mushrooms are usually bought in powder form and are used primarily as a nutritional supplement. They can be added to smoothies, warm drinks and baking recipes.

RICE MALT SYRUP
Rice malt syrup is derived from brown rice and is a readily available fructose-free alternative sweetener to sugar. It has a low glycemic index, which means it releases energy at a slower and more sustained rate and won't lead to a sugar rush. It is also easier to metabolise than regular sugar and may be used instead of regular sugar in recipes.

TAHINI
A paste made from hulled or unhulled sesame seeds, tahini contains magnesium, protein, potassium, iron, calcium, vitamins B and E. It is high in unsaturated fat, also known as 'good fat'.

Tahini is commonly used to make hummus and is a great base for sauces, dressings or an alternative to butter or margarine.

TURMERIC
Turmeric is part of the ginger family and contains curcumin, an active ingredient that has potent anti-inflammatory properties and is high in antioxidants. Curcumin isn't easily absorbed into the bloodstream, however, and is best consumed with black pepper to increase the absorption of curcumin's superior health benefits. Dried ground turmeric is commonly used in curries, soups, smoothies and hot drinks.

ACKNOWLEDGEMENTS

WE WOULD LIKE TO THANK:

Toly and Alexis, for your love, support and patience.

Melissa Kayser, Marg Bowman, Kate Armstrong and everyone else at Hardie Grant Publishing for your help and support in bringing this book to life and for giving us this amazing opportunity.

Kate Daniel, for your indispensable guidance and wealth of knowledge.

Dixon Patton, for your beautiful artwork.

Auntie Larissa, for first putting a paintbrush into Lily's hand.

Nana Peg, for your never-ending love and support.

Jirra Lulla Harvey, for your ongoing support and for being a constant source of inspiration.

Alison Ravenscroft, for your warmth. and encouragement.

Outback Pride Fresh, for sustainably growing so many of the wonderful bushfoods this country has to offer and The Vegetable Connection in Fitzroy, Melbourne, for supplying them.

INDEX

Published in 2017 by Hardie Grant Explore,
a division of Hardie Grant Publishing

Hardie Grant Explore (Melbourne)
Wurundjeri Country
Building 1, 658 Church Street
Richmond, Victoria 3121

Hardie Grant Explore (Sydney)
Gadigal Country
Level 7, 45 Jones Street
Ultimo, NSW 2007

www.hardiegrant.com/au/explore

All rights reserved. No part of this publication may be reproduced, stored in a retrieval system or transmitted in any form by any means, electronic, mechanical, photocopying, recording or otherwise, without the prior written permission of the publishers and copyright holders.

The moral rights of the author have been asserted.

Copyright text, illustrations and photography © Lily Alice and Thomas O'Quinn 2017
Copyright Indigenous artwork © Dixon Patten
Copyright concept and design © Hardie Grant Publishing 2017

A catalogue record for this book is available from the National Library of Australia

Hardie Grant acknowledges the Traditional Owners of the Country on which we work, the Wurundjeri people of the Kulin Nation and the Gadigal people of the Eora Nation, and recognises their continuing connection to the land, waters and culture. We pay our respects to their Elders past and present.

Australian Bush Superfoods
ISBN 9781741175400

10 9

Commissioning editor
Melissa Kayser

Managing editor
Marg Bowman

Project editor
Kate J. Armstrong, Megan Cuthbert

Design and botanical illustrations
dreamsandbones.com.au

Additional artwork
Dixon Patten

Editor
Kate Daniel

Proofreader
Kate J. Armstrong

Index
Max McMaster

Production Manager
Todd Rechner

Pre-press
Megan Ellis, Splitting Image Colour Studio

Printed in China by LEO Paper Group LTD.

The paper this book is printed on is certified against the Forest Stewardship Council® Standards and other sources. FSC® promotes environmentally responsible, socially beneficial and economically viable management of the world's forests.